Song of Solomon For Lovers

...bringing back healthy and wholesome discussions and portrayals of sex

Gary McFarlane

Copyright © 2014 Gary McFarlane

All rights reserved.

ISBN-10: 1499145357
ISBN-13: 978-1499145359

Expanded and reprinted August 2014

Cover Design
SelfPubBookCovers.com/FrinaArt

DEDICATION

To all couples who are married
and desire to experience that John 10: 10
assurance of fullness and excess
in their sexual relationship;
as well as to all singles who desire
to prepare for their future
John 10: 10 sexual fullness and excess.

CONTENT

Introduction   8

PART ONE

Chapter 1   13
What are the issues?

Chapter 2   20
Do the Children really need to know that?

Chapter 3   32
When love and sex goes wrong.

Chapter 4   41
Singles, sex, the Bible, marriages and their issues (1)

Chapter 5   60
Singles, sex, the Bible, marriages and their issues (2)

Chapter 6   74
Singles, sex, the Bible, marriages and their issues (3)

Chapter 7   89
Sin and Iniquity

Chapter 8   107
Belief theories in CBT

Chapter 9   123
The Change process

Chapter 10 134
Prep for oneness: Pre-marriage Prep

Chapter 11 144
Sex Therapy

Chapter 12 154
What happens during each sexual response cycle?

Chapter 13 160
What is Sex Addiction?

Chapter 14 176
Errors of Pastoral workers

PART TWO

Chapter 15 190
Song of Solomon as a pattern for lovers

Chapter 16 201
The 5 loves demonstrated by the couple (1)

Chapter 17 214
The 5 loves demonstrated by the couple (2)

Epilogue 232

Reference List 237

My inspiration comes from a loving family,
Particularly my wife Cynthia and four children
(how did that happen!),
Pierce, Mia-Claire, Abigail and the one just come forth
(Xavier).

ACKNOWLEDGMENTS

Great and awesome God Almighty. My Father, my mentor, my compassionate Good Shepherd, my all in all.
The Great I Am
&
Cynthia, my pillow mate.

Song of Solomon For Lovers

...bringing back healthy and wholesome discussions and portrayal of sex

Introduction

Sexuality as an important part of human sexual functioning

The Church has been a significant contributor to the church attenders evolving sexuality (including dysfunctions). Church leaders have been very good at saying "no, no, no" when couples are not married and then "yes, yes, yes" when they get married. They have not, however, been very good at "how, how, how?" when guidance is needed.

We live in a sex-saturated, sex crazed, sex obsessed society. Little wonder people are continually searching for intimacy which is found at its height when expressed in the "oneness" with one another that God designed. In the same consistent manner in which people seek to satisfy the yearning that there is something or someone outside of oneself which is, or who is, more omnipotent and omniscient than them; so it is they search for a form of sex to satisfy a yearning.

The fact is that man is hardwired with a desire to get back inside. Inside the womb it was safe, warm, peaceful, restful, responsibility free, contented – like few other places experienced since entering this world. Why not at a deep unconscious level try to get back that feeling once experienced? Human sexual dysfunction arises from either physical or psychological factors; sex therapy is mainly concerned with the latter.

The old testament book of Song of Solomon (also called Song of Songs) has been allegorized so that the sexual content is mostly ignored. At best, it is a book in the Bible that is dipped into for a few pointers. Song of Solomon is a sexual book and is an excellent template for lovers.

This is what some say about Song of Solomon:

"Inspired by God to be included in the Bible and the only entire collection devoted exclusively to courtship and marriage."

"Best romance story ever written"

"Inspiring, erotic, very steamy"

"I was shocked and thrilled that it was so explicit and erotic in talking about sex."

"This book gave me permission to be wild and crazy with my husband in bed"

Despite Solomon's later failures, God chose him to portray love and sex as He designed it. Therefore it is for us to make some sense and understanding of its application to us. It is an instruction book on love and sex within marriage.

In this book, I endeavour to identify what it looks like when sex has the following attributes:

- When it is not working
- When it wants to work
- An examination of the things that get in the way and stop it working
- Preparation for your time when you move from singleness
- When sex is a bother and a chore
- When sex is not what it says on the tin
- When sex is fake
- When sex is a burden and not a pleasure

I also look for the solutions to the following statements:

- "Must we…?"
- "I've got a headache…Me too"
- "I do"…but not to sex!
- "I don't know what all the fuse and hype is about…"
- "The earth does not shake for me"

- "Gadgets aren't helping"

Finally, I attempt to provide insight into the following:

- Where do we go for help with our sex life?
- What or who is a sex therapist? Or is it a sexologist or a psychosexual therapist?
- What are the factors which indicate the possible need for sex therapy?
- Sex addiction and love addiction
- Song of Solomon as a pattern for lovers which works
- Sex needs a helping hand

God's grace is all sufficient to forgive us of our sins and to cleanse us from all unrighteousness (1 John 1: 9).

The new born enters life with innocence and a brain ready to receive its first data of life's experiences. Mostly that comes from the family of origin into which we are born. Those experiences are shaping life; a distorted image develops. The individual distorted image of male and female come together to form a partnership, a relationship, to marry and become one. These two distorted images are supposed to live a lifetime together in harmony! However, this experience is often far from tranquil. Only God can restore both broken and distorted images and reshape them, as he would have them. Experiences from the five senses create experiences and memories (whether conscious or unconscious), and as that happens, negative experiences can cause the person to gain a distorted image.

A thorough understanding and application of five loves, is essential to rebuilding the damaged relationship of marriage. Historically the Greek language used at least five words precisely and quite distinctly to describe the various facets of love. By looking at each of those different word descriptions we can build up the identifying features of all the components that the word *love* should contain and how these should be demonstrated in all healthy, progressive and fulfilling relationships. Those five words for love are **Epithumia, Eros, Phileo, Storge** and **Agape**.

> *Let's learn the truth so that the truth may set us free (John 8: 32)*

...rather than untruth continuing to keep us in bondage. The truth can be liberating. (For some though, it can appear like a greater bondage). The truth can lead us to repentance and a changed life style.

PART ONE

Chapter 1

What are the issues?

In this chapter several fictional case scenarios are outlined to raise the questions: are there any issues which are readily identifiable from any of these scenarios, which might point to the need for sex therapy? Do your sexual issues resonate with any features of these case illustrations?

Case 1

Sarah and Simon are distressed because Simon is not able to maintain an erection reliably enough to have sex that is satisfying for both. Sarah has reached menopause and, as such, thinks that Simon cannot maintain his erection because he does not fancy her anymore. Since her father had an affair and eventually left her mother, she also believes that Simon is having an affair and will leave her.

Her view is that they should not need sex therapy because if Simon really loves her and is not having an affair, they would not have a problem.

Case 2

Sheila has gone off sex. She had been doing it out of obligation since the birth of their third child. Ted has not been pressuring her for more sex. Late one evening after falling asleep for a while, she went downstairs and found him groaning in a room with his hands in his trousers watching porn on his PC. She was devastated.

Case 3

Kim was two years married when Jim came home at lunchtime to surprise her and found her in the bathroom pleasuring herself. He had listened at the door for a while and was surprised at the extent of her noises and enjoyment. She is always very quiet and placid when they make love. They make love twice per week.

She was brought up in a strict religious home and believes that female masturbation is very bad, but she learnt to do it at university and has not been able to stop since then. She just could not share such a secret with Jim. She believes it would be wrong to seek more sex with Jim as she believes he would look down on her and think she wants sex too excessively. He might become threatened by her needs.

Case 4

Jane has been married for 6 months. Their honeymoon was a disaster in the bedroom. She was a virgin when they married but she read some books and friends had given her some advice before the wedding. When John tried to penetrate her, it was painful and she could not relax.

She is up tight each time they go to bed. She wants to have sex, but cannot relax enough for him to get his penis inside her. They have tried repeatedly, but end up mutually stimulating each other. They are so very much in love and want to have penetrative sex.

Case 5

Janet does not think that she has ever had an orgasm. She gets very turned on, but has not experienced the intense build up which ends in the very pleasurable muscular sensations which she would describe as an orgasm. She knows there is something else, but is scared to let go and be out of control when the sensations build to a high level. She feels like she will wet herself if she lets go. How embarrassing if she did pee herself during sex! How would she live with that?

Case 6

Stephanie experiences intense pain when Jack tries to penetrate her during sex. Her body goes tense as it anticipates pain and expects it to hurt. When he gets in, it is tight and this also hurts. Afterwards she is left with a burning sensation. On her own, she can put a finger inside her vagina and so cannot understand why she experiences such pain from Jack.

Case 7

Marcia and Ben have both been married before to other partners. They have been married for a little over a year. Ben had first married when aged 19, to his first girlfriend from school, but she divorced him after 4 years and he learned that she had been cheating on him. He now knows that he had always suffered from coming too quickly – called premature ejaculation.

His first wife had been understanding or so he thought. He could never help her to have an orgasm when he penetrated her. He came within just a few thrusts and was never in control or able to prolong it. The problem has continued into his second marriage and he fears losing Marcia the same way.

Case 8

Malcolm lost his father to a heart attack 6 months ago. He is depressed and taking medication. There are numerous members of his family who suffer from hypertension. He reduced his salt intake but that made no difference to his high blood pressure and so his doctor has commenced him on drugs to control it. Within months of taking the antidepressant and hypertension medication, Malcolm realised he had not had sex with his wife for 6 months and still had no desire to do so.

He put it out of his mind until he noticed how angrily and out of context he responded to his wife when she approached him lovingly for sex. Two months after that episode he recognised that he could no longer get an erection and the few times when he does, it is short-lived and he is certainly not able to sustain it to penetration. He is getting even more depressed and cannot figure out what has changed and caused his erectile difficulties.

Case 9

Percy and Elizabeth were both widowed 25 and 28 years ago respectively. Both are in their early 70's and have not been sexually active for 15 years. They have been married for one year now, but find their sex life is not compatible and have different levels of desire for sex. They don't know what to do to satisfy each other because their physiology has changed and the way their bodies react to stimulation seems different to the past.

Case 10

John and Emma have suffered the loss of their 3 year old from a road traffic accident. The accident also resulted in John losing both legs above the knee, when he had to be cut free; he also lost an arm. He now has prosthesis fitted and is adjusting to their use. No one in the hospital has asked him much about sex and how or if they will be able to resume their sex life following the accident, due to the trauma, the treatment, living with the prosthesis' and an element of post traumatic stress. His mind is willing to try to have sex, but his disability means learning all over again.

Case 11

Joshua and Louise are getting married in two months. They are both virgins and have never dated anyone else or had any type of sexual contact with the opposite sex. They are from a strict religious sect and their minister would be very unhappy if they sought information from outside the organisation. They do not know how to consummate their marriage or what to do. They have never had much more than very basic sex education.

A sound of silence and the unheard plea for sexual help is often visible in folks described above. Their dilemmas sometimes have a "yuk" factor and they know society frowns on them having any sexual outlet and that keeps them muted from voicing a sexual need.

> *"I have cancer. I am terminally ill. I am severely disabled. I am very elderly; but I still feel sexual or want to feel sexual and want to express my sexual feelings to my partner."*

Even if full-blown sex therapy is not indicated in all of these cases above, most of the individuals could and would benefit from some sex therapy education information.

Sex addiction and love addiction are increasingly prominent problems being faced by an increasing number of people. Love addiction is not yet widely recognised by society. It will be headline news that someone can become addicted to the social media.

The man and the woman, each with their distorted images from the different environments from which they have come, are to become one and live in harmony together as they become man and wife. In many instances, that is just not going to happen without some help. The single distorted image is waiting to find their distorted image in order to become one with that person. It is God Who restores the broken and distorted images and reshapes them, as He would have them.

Chapter 2

Do the children really need to know all that?

CHILDREN LEARN WHAT THEY LIVE

If a child lives with criticism

He learns to condemn

If a child lives with hostility

He learns to fight

If a child lives with ridicule

He learns to be shy

If a child lives with shame

He learns to feel guilty

If a child lives with tolerance

He learns to be patient

If a child lives with encouragement

He learns confidence.

If a child lives with praise

He learns to appreciate

If a child lives with fairness

He learns justice

If a child lives with security

He learns to have faith

If a child lives with approval

He learns to like himself

If a child lives with acceptance and friendship

He learns to find love in the world

Dorothy Law Nolte[1]

(Remember that the child soon becomes the man or woman. What will he or she pass on?)

Developmental history from childhood

Education sits alongside social, emotional, moral and cognitive development. Children develop at different rates. Growth spurts and plateaus, heredity and environmental factors all have substantial contributions. Sex education has to be considered in the context of child developmental patterns – a time of potential greatest impact and influence.

Since the mid 1990's we have had very concrete and persuasive scientific evidence that the teen brain is immature and functions differently from an adult. Their brain does not reach full maturity until the third decade of life. The prefrontal cortex (PFC) is the last area to develop and is the brains centre for reasoning, judgment, self-evaluation and planning. It suppresses impulses and makes decisions rationally, weighing up the pros and cons, alongside consequences. Since that part of the brain is not fully mature until mid-twenties, the CYP is susceptible to the amygdala (a principle structure of the "feeling" brain) that has matured. The amygdala is more short-sighted, emotion driven and thus susceptible to coercion and peer pressure.

The phase of childhood from birth to age 6 is a critical time of sensitivity, during which time templates are created which shape future interpersonal interactions. Many people experience wounding during their early development and learn to numb their pain by self-soothing. Those behaviour traits, which are practiced from childhood, become the hallmark traits which the adult may continue to struggle with as it may become a compulsive behaviour in adulthood; be it a critical tongue, a repetitive practice of stealing, being a loner, using and misusing such things as alcohol, drugs, spending, food, sex, relationships, or the internet.

All compulsive behaviours feature a very complex **emotional** and **biochemical process** that has origins in childhood trauma and the deprivation of authentic intimacy and bonding during early development. We know that maladaptive (inappropriate) responses to learned behaviours then start to appear between the ages of 4 and 9. Add to that the onset of sexual imprinting taking place from age 3 to 4 and peaking at 8 to 9, with an upper tail at about aged 13, a map and template for living life is carved out. These ways of having relationships, which includes the early formation of sexual relating, are becoming templates and become activated at puberty and develop and continue throughout adult life.

Here are examples of how parents can unwittingly set up poor sexual templates for a child:

- Neglecting to monitor and reinforce healthy sexual rehearsal play.
- Punishing or humiliating children for their rehearsal play.
- Prematurely inducting children into sexual rehearsal play.
- Coercing children into age-discrepant sexual rehearsal play.

Sexual Map & Sexual Template

The new born baby starts life in innocence with the brain having little data. Then the five senses deposit messages and shaping begins. Negative experiences cause distortion and this distorted image continues to be knocked about and shaped by events in our lives.

A love map is an individuals unique erotic signature. We take in experiences (good, indifferent and bad) as we journey in our families and take from the family scripts for how to live life. That sexual map contains our likes, dislikes, preferences, inhibits, erotic signature and such things, which we may not even be conscious of having, until the right circumstance triggers them.

The sexual map becomes fixed at a point and becomes the sexual template by which we live out our sex life, unless we later seek to change aspects of it – often with help. That sexual map evolves from childhood.

The new born baby that becomes the man or woman

When sex education in school is age inappropriate, we store up tremendous potential problems for a future generation. Let us consider the impact of sex education on the sexuality and sexual expression of children and young people (CYP).

CYP viewing and being exposed to information, which is too explicit for the age and maturity of the young person, can be traumatic. Such early contact with sexual information, that is too much and too soon, can have an emotional impact on their later sexual experience and development. This may contribute to sexual dysfunctions and problems in later sexual relationships. Sex education is often the first such exposure to material which is too explicit. In Britain, sex education has enabled such a prospect to be a reality.

Sexually explicit material (and here I am referring to material that is too much too such – rather than very explicit per se) can cause trauma. That trauma can be at work in a subtle and unconscious way, but in time it sets the CYP on a path towards increased vulnerability to sexual compulsive and addictive disorders.

Even if sexual dysfunction does not manifest in later life, other issues may have an increased prevalence and potential. The visual imprint, which is carving out the sexual template, has a long exposure time in the brain, leaving an impression that may be activated adversely in the future. It may also have normalised thinking about what the image depicted and set up sex myths which are acted upon as truths.

More controversially is the biological vulnerability argument - that young girl's cervix is only one cell thick. As such it is easily penetrated by the human papillomavirus that can cause cervical cancer (although a vaccination is now available). Only the maturing process of time allows the surface of the cervix to develop 30 to 40 layers, making penetration more difficult. Delaying sexual intercourse is a strong indicator that is advanced within this "biological vulnerability" argument.

Age appropriate or is it pornography?

There is a fast changing landscape where the personal computer has increased prevalence in the education syllabus from an earlier age. Many websites, that are recommended, are being viewed without parental monitoring. There are a wealth of publications that are endorsed and so are being viewed as acceptable reading material. Many of those NHS and Department of Education endorsed literature and website material can be classed as being "too much too soon" and predispose many CYP's to future sexual dysfunctions, including sex addiction. The government acknowledges that CYP are being pushed into grown-up territory well before their time.

There are those who ask whether some current sex education material is so graphic as to be hazardous to a child's health and pose a rhetorical question by asking "you're teaching my child, what?" Dr Miriam Grossman is one such person and that question is the title of her book, which is entitled: *You're teaching my child what?* She and others challenge the premise that CYP are completely capable of making responsible sexual decisions and can think through complex issues, plan ahead and consider consequences; referring to their restricted brain development which affects decision making. They point to the CYP's lack of judgment (due to their young age).

If the first exposure to sexually explicit material, even in the guise of sex education, is age inappropriate or age indigestible, it can be a link to future sex addiction. Normalising and desensitisation to explicit material takes place too soon, which sets up CYP for future relational sexual dysfunctions and mental health issues. In their book called "The Porn Trap", Larry & Wendy Maltz say that:

"If you have issues with porn today, chances are they can be trace back to your early encounters with pornography. Childhood is a formative and vulnerable period in a person's life, a time when our attitudes are shaped and many of our behaviours take root".[2]

Frequent news stories include the following:

"A sexual disaster for teenagers and society…sharp rise in teenage pregnancy."[3]

"This is the first generation growing up seeing rape before even losing their virginity..." [4]

"Boys swap sex sites at break time..." [5]

"Even 10 year olds post pictures of themselves in their underwear..." [6]

"Between 60-90% of under 16's have viewed hardcore online porn" [7]

"Teens are spending on average 1 hour 40 minutes per week (87 hours per year) viewing online porn. The single largest group of Internet porn consumers is children aged 12-17" [8]

"[There has been a] dramatic increase in young girls using the Internet to become amateur porn stars. Porn is equated with sexual training and a manual. Desensitization to sexually explicit porn is taking place in an ever younger age. Girls view porn to check out others girls and normalise own sexual behaviour and attitudes" [9]

Sexual templates are unconsciously created from youth and will contribute to possible sexual dysfunctions, including sex addiction. We know that CYP see their first porn by aged 9-11 and the single largest porn group users are aged 12-17. 60-90% of under 16's have viewed online porn and teens are spending on average 1-hour 40mins per week viewing online porn, with the primary focus being masturbation. Addictive and excessive masturbation then sets them up for continued false intimacy, rather than sex in relationships with real people. Instead many prefer cybersex.

Consequences of too much too soon

In their early years development, CYP are getting a secure base for living life and gaining future relationship interactions from their computer, mobile phone and other gadgets, rather than from the attachment to a mother figure. Gadgets are becoming the surrogate significant "other person" in the CYP's life. Those gadgets create new allegiances and reliance, so that "false intimacies" are created with these gadgets, which then substitute real person relationships, and cybersex becomes even more prevalent.

In the USA porn addiction is described as the newest and most challenging mental health problem: the issue is whether sex education will play a role in limiting the current and next generation of CYP becoming one of those statistics or if sex education unwittingly contributing.

A key issue is when legitimate sex education stops and porn begins. That was the subject of controversy surrounding a Channel 4 show "The joy of teen sex", which was branded as porn by Mediawatch UK in January 2011[10]. It was deemed to have crossed the line into prurience, with graphic scenes of sex that can only be described as pornographic. Whilst the show claimed to offer sex advice to under 18's, it airs after the watershed.

Many parents are abdicating sex education responsibility and leaving it to schools, peers, the internet, library and other mediums as their main (and sometimes only) source of sex education. That leaves CYP with deficits in their knowledge. They fill in the deficits with information from the sources that take on truth and dogma, long enough for damage to be done - at a time when the brain is not yet fully developed. Misinformation, sexual myths and reluctance to seek third person authoritative input compounds the psychological factors that lead to sexual dysfunction and addictions.

Britain has the highest rate of teenage pregnancy in Western Europe[11], and there is increased sexually transmitted infection amongst CYP. Both of those factors make it a disincentive to reduce available material. After all, few are monitoring the prevalence of subsequent sexual dysfunctions which CYP later present within sex therapy.

Sex therapy beckons for many more couples at an earlier stage in their relationships because of the exposure being at an even younger age than was experienced by a past generation. Predisposing and precipitating factors are increasingly evident in their experiences.

Sex education should be an integrated education process that is developmentally appropriate, truly evidence-based and the relative explicit content taught age appropriately, as the CYP develops through the school years. Parents need to take a more active role in reviewing sex education material available to CYP to ensure age appropriate viewing and learning within the sex education curriculum.

Chapter 3

When love and sex goes wrong

A sexual craving has a strong pull and it desires to be satisfied; a pleasure craving is so strong that it can override cognitive, logical reasoning processes. We can see the force of such a craving from the life of a number of characters in the Bible. Samson is one of them, but let us look at a lesser known character and the power of sexual craving and desire upon his life. 2 Samuel 13 introduces us to one of King David's sons, called Amnon. He worked himself up into a frenzy of passion and desire for his half sister called Tamar.

Once he had dined on desire and lust for so long, it was going to be difficult for him to pull back from seeking to fulfil that desire and lust. We see where he is at in 2 Sam 13: 1 – 6.

Amnon finds someone who bolsters up his bad thinking in the form of Jonadab – a cousin. He was a very crafty man and as such will have carved out a practice of risk taking at others expense. The act of being crafty will always be at someone else's expense. The voice of bad reasoning (coming from such a friend) endorses Amnon's bad thinking (2 Sam 13: 5).

How far did his best friend and cousin think Amnon would go in order to satisfy his lust? He did not seem to be concerned that his encouragement would result in Amnon raping his half sister – Tamar. His focus was to be there for his friend and not be concerned about consequences to others.

Understand that Amnon is in the cycle of "acting out", by acting upon his urges to the detriment of consequences. The course of acting out includes deceiving his father (King David), whom he knows to be a wise and knowledgeable man. He thinks he has got one over on him. In truth, it is all exciting and titillating stuff. The scheme to get King David to come to see him is a part of an adrenaline producing excitement; yet a very risky scheme to pretend to be ill when he knew that he could be found out by a wise king, with wise advisors. Will he and his scheme be discovered? The risk taking is adrenaline pumping, oxytocin and dopamine secreting highs, which take Amnon into his own false world? His logical, adult cognitive reasoning processes are taken offline during this hormone secreting period which takes him on a high - with disastrous consequences looming in the real world which he has momentarily left.

He is enjoying the pleasures of his high state of euphoria and enhancing the forthcoming fulfilment of his desires. By playing with desire, fantasy and lust, he is producing oxytocin, dopamine and other chemical reaction in the brain which are swamping and feeding the brain's pleasure zone, meaning very powerful effects are taking place in the brain. This stage in his acting out is the most pleasurable element and often more so than fulfilling the actual desire of sex.

David had unknowingly ruled himself out as the one who could stop the plot. Indeed it could be said that it is David's very act that set up this sequence of events, because of the effects of iniquity visiting his children from his past. His own sexual sin with Bathsheba had meant David had pronounced a generational curse upon himself. When replying to Nathan the prophet immediately after his own adultery with Bathsheba, in 2 Samuel 12: 5, David says: " ..*the man who has done this...he shall restore fourfold for the lamb"*. This much later event, involving his own son Amnon, is the fulfilment of one of fourfold punishments David called down upon his own head.

Having got Tamar to his house, the climax is building for Amnon and is unstoppable. The adult thinking and logical reasoning side of his brain is swamped by self-producing biochemicals secreted into the pleasure receptacles of his brain. They have the effect of overriding logical thought, such that the drive to have his sexual desire fulfilled is unstoppable and rape is inevitable.

It is very different for Tamar. We see the adult logical cognitive reasoning side of the brain at work in her. Her thinking is unhindered; she thinks ahead. She considers consequences of what Amnon plans to do and offers alternative solutions in 2 Samuel 13: 12-13. That is what the adult thinking and reasoning brain does when given a chance and is not hampered. She tries to reason with him. All that she says makes logical, reasoned sense and should be heeded.

Amnon is not able to reason with her. The feeling, pleasurable brain overrides the cognitive; it has swamped the cognitive side and pleasure fulfilment rules supreme, meaning his discipline is lost and his own values have been trampled upon. Amnon is too far gone as that side of his brain is shut down. His discipline has gone and his feelings take over, begging to be met. They demand, "give me", "feed me", "fulfil me", "I must have it".

Immediate gratification is a trait of sex addiction. His heightened arousal drives the eyes, hands and feet to do its bidding and any thoughts of later consequence is quelled. The acting out looks only to the "here and now". The feeling brain is content to drive the eyes, hands, feet and indeed all of the body in order to comply with the pursuit of pleasure; blow the consequence! Postpone thoughts about the consequence; enjoy the here and now; there is no future that needs thinking about right now.

Amnon's immediate response is what we see in 2 Samuel 13: 14, as he overpowers and rapes Tamar. He is not able to hear her words because they do not register. This inability to keep control was dominated by the power of his desire, thinking and need to fulfil and satisfy the build up of infatuation. Her words did not enter the cognitive reasoning and processing side of his brain. All that he heard was talk coming from Tamar's mouth, but not her words.

There is a distinct difference between "hearing" and "listening". Hearing is the act of causing the ears to receive noise. Listening is an active processing within the brain, where the words it hears are processed and decisions made as to what the content means and whether anything needs to be done with what was spoken.

Amnon rapes Tamar, such is the strength of desire. Consider his response immediately after desire has been satisfied. The biochemical effects are wearing off and equilibrium is returning to normal functioning. Cognitive reasoning is now back online. In 2 Sam 13: 14 – 15 we see the contrast between a man overcome by desire, compared to a man now exercising logical reasoning. A strong hatred is the aftermath of desire satisfied. He is now experiencing the aftermath of the consequences to decisions taken and acted upon. After feelings are satisfied, there is an immediate kick back. Biochemicals in the brain dissipate and logical cognitive reasoning breaks through and surfaces. Consequences and repercussions can be seen.

The immediate aftermath is one of Amnon hating Tamar; hatred that is stronger than the love he first had for her. How can that be?! How can love change to hatred so quickly? It was not ever love, but lust. This was love defiled; this is Epithumia defiled and distorted.

Infatuation, love craze, self-induced obsession, addiction to desire fulfilment (which, by the way ran, generationally through his family lineage), were drivers in Amnon. Call it what you will, but it was not the love that is described throughout this book and certainly not one of the five loves. Those healthy types of love do not function in the way manifested by Amnon, as love cannot be turned on and off in an instant.

Amnon sexually assaulted Tamar. That is how far desire for sexual pleasure - unrestrained - can take a person and beyond. Poor decisions and judgments turn to bad choices, resulting from wrong thinking, which have their roots at times in past generational iniquity. Added to them was the suspect company from whom Amnon received poor advice. He failed to take captive his imaginings, which were allowed to roam free and unhindered. The fantasies demanded satisfaction and it cost him dearly. Sin will always cost us more than we had bargained for and were willing to pay. It reaps a high price.

Amnon's actions ultimately caused loss of his life at the hands of one of his half brothers. The victim (his half sister) was left with a life long trauma which had far reaching effects for her future.

When your reference point is not the Lord, a couple has a very serious problem. It is said that Abraham Lincoln was asked if he was sure that God was on his side. He replied, *"I haven't thought much about it. I just want to know I'm on God's side"*. See the difference? Learn the difference. Implement that difference. Practice that difference. Ensure it is the cornerstone in your relationship.

Make very sure it is practiced in your individual life. The voice which you hear, the voice which you heed, is it God's voice or your voice? Test it and see and so ensure you are confident that God is on your side. Where a servant's heart is evidently manifested and present, you can be sure you are on the right track.

Be sure that it is not in fact you trying to get God on your side. Use Psalms 26: 1 – 3 as another of your templates against which to assess and judge your actions, whilst in the place of conflict. Ask the Lord to cross-examine you, to test your motives and affections. It will show up whether you have indeed taken His loving kindness and truth as your ideals.

In a place of conflict you should be able to say to the Lord, "I don't have a plan Lord". You should remain malleable and pliable in His hands. You should be clay on the potter's wheel, available to be directed and molded with the circumstances, as He directs you.

To sum up then, we should always ensure that after drifting away from Him being in charge, we return to the implementing and practice of Prov 3: 5 – 6.

> *"Trust in the Lord with all your **heart and lean not on your own understanding**. In all your ways acknowledge Him and He **shall** direct your paths".*

Note that *"paths"* is plural and not singular. He will direct all your ways. That is a future tense; and so He will direct your ways in the future so that His way is a lamp; a lamp onto our feet and a light on your path - Psalms 119: 105. Such a lamp does not glow bright into the future. It shines as a light only so far ahead, sufficient to see your next step and no further. That means you become wholly reliant on God for your next step, nothing more, nothing further into the future. You are wholly reliant upon Him.

We have enough information to indicate that other characters, like Samson, had a problem with desire and lust. Samson saw; he wanted, he demanded, he sought self-satisfaction, he took. They are traits of compulsivity, even if not truly addicted.

In the Amnon example above we gain insight into what goes wrong when all of the five loves are not working well in the couple relationship. Later on we take a look at sex at its best and when it is working without dysfunctions and as the Creator designed it to work. We take a snapshot view of a period in the life of Solomon and the woman who was to become his bride and lover – the Shulamith. We look at Song of Solomon as a place where we can learn many lessons and maybe obviate the need for a sex therapist.

Chapter 4

Singles, Sex, the Bible, Marriage and their issues (1)

Singles, do these thoughts cross your mind from time to time?

- Single…but not my choice
- God, you've done this to me
- Unwanted gift-take it back
- What does it mean to be "single" in this generation?
- No way! She/He is like a sister/brother to me. We grew up together in the same youth group and Church!
- Have I set an insurmountable standard that needs revisiting?
- Facts & Figures
- Some truths: What the media didn't tell you
- Shifting standards and moving the goal posts of acceptability of what we can and cannot do
- What's the problem with the literature that I read and my use of technology?
- Can't see a problem with the teens magazines, women's magazines and books that I read!
- The latest best seller "Fifty shades of Grey": What's the fuss about?
- Men's magazines and their books: Soft porn? What?
- Cybernet and internet: (Chat rooms, blogging, webcam)

- Pornography
- Learning from Sampson and Jephthah. How not to do it!
- What am I digesting and how does it reverberate upon me?
- Defining sex in this generation: when is "sex", sex?
- It's an age thing: life stages
- Unevenly yoked: but better than being s.....
- What is it with men and commitment anyway?
- Self-pleasuring: A role, no role, therapeutic or just wrong? Can't keep the promise not to do it again? Flashbacks just before communion?
- Self-condemnation is worse than the act
- Intimacy: "I'm scared"
- How far is too far?
- I want to know what love is
- Me and my view of God, determines my relationship with others!
- Intimacy with God as a prelude to right intimacy with others?
- The past, living in the present and informing the future?
- Family Scripts: "Why do I do the things I don't want to do…?"
- Developing Body, Mind and Spirit
- Renewing the mind. But how does the commendation in the book of Romans actually work?
- The five Loves

- Enhancing relationships through communication skills
- Self-Concept, Self image, Self esteem
- Song of Solomon in context, with a health warning
- Don't awaken love and desire, "…but what if it is awakened?"
- It happens at 3 in the morning?
- What do I do with all those powerful feelings?

Are we duped into marriage as the preferred status?

Here is a quote from taken from **Blue-Eyes, Brown-Eyes: The Experiment that Shocked the Nation and Turned a Town Against its Most Famous Daughter**, *By Stephen G. Bloom (Stephen-g-bloom@uiowa.edu):*

"How do you think it would feel to be a Negro boy or girl?" Jane asked, her teacher-eyes widening on cue. "It would be hard to know, wouldn't it, unless we actually experienced discrimination ourselves." Jane pulled out the armbands and asked each of the blue-eyed kids to wear one. "Would you like to find out?"

A chorus of "Yeah!" went up. Jane took a deep breath, and went to work. Seventeen blue- eyed children were set apart from eight children with brown eyes and three with green eyes.

"The brown-eyed people are the better people in this room," Jane started. "They are cleaner and they are smarter."

"Aw, they are not," Alan Moss said, maybe more to break the silence than for anything else.

"Oh, yes, they are," Jane intoned, making eye contact with each student. "Brown-eyed people are smarter than blue-eyed people."

Even though they hung on her every word, Jane knew instinctively that the children weren't going to buy her pitch unless she came up with a reason, the more "scientific" to these space-age children of the sixties, the better.

"Eye color, hair color and skin color are caused by a chemical," Jane proclaimed, picking up a stick of chalk and writing in large block letters MELANIN on the blackboard. Jane knew the moment she touched the chalk to the slate board her comments would become official. That sound of contact made what she was saying real. Melanin, Jane lectured, is what causes intelligence. The more melanin, the darker the person - and the smarter the person. "Brown-eyed people have more of that chemical in their eyes, so brown-eyed people are better than those with blue eyes," Jane said. "Blue-eyed people sit around and do nothing. You give them something nice and they just wreck it."

There were uneasy stares and within seconds Jane realized that a palpable change had overtaken her students. Jane saw an immediate chasm dividing the blue-eyed kids from the rest. Jane was poised to make that chasm as wide as her kids would allow. "Do blue-eyed people remember what they've been taught?" Jane asked, and automatically, the brown-eyed kids responded "No!" Jane rattled off the list of rules for the day, which included the requirement that blue-eyed kids use paper cups if they insisted on drinking from the water fountain.

"Why?" brown-eyed Debbie Anderson asked haltingly.

"Because we might catch something," came the swift response from Ricky Ring.

Everyone looked towards Mrs. Elliott, and all Jane had to do was nod her head, so it must be true...If eyes (no matter what color they are) are *windows to the mind, then Jane Elliott had given herself the ultimate power of looking into 28 souls that day. She wasn't quite sure what she had unleashed. The empowered brown-eyes kids proceeded to berate their blue-eyed classmates. They were merciless. "Well, what do you expect from him, Mrs. Elliott," one brown-eyed student said as a blue-eyed student got an arithmetic problem wrong. "He's a bluey!"*[12].

Headline in The Huffington Post on 29 January 2014 reads: **"Short People May Experience Feelings Of Inferiority, Research Suggests"**. Here are some quotes from the article:

"Scientists used virtual reality technology to reduce the height of volunteers travelling on a computer-simulated Tube train by 10in (25cm)....The experience of being shorter increased reports of negative feelings, such as being incompetent, dislikeable or inferior....Professor Daniel Freeman, who led the Medical Research Council-funded study, said: "Being tall is associated with greater career and relationship success".

"Height is taken to convey authority, and we feel taller when we feel more powerful. It is little wonder then that men and women tend to over-report their height...In this study we reduced people's height, which led to a striking consequence: people felt inferior and this caused them to feel overly mistrustful. This all happened in a virtual reality simulation, but we know that people behave in VR as they do in real life".

"It provides a key insight into paranoia, showing that people's excessive mistrust of others directly builds upon their own negative feelings about themselves...The results were very clear: lowering of height led to more

negative evaluations of the self compared with others and greater levels of paranoia," said the scientists writing in the journal Psychiatry Research".

What if society has conditioned us to believe that "Married" is better and that "Singleness" is a lesser state and one to be shunned and moved out of, in preference for the status of marriage or being in a union? What if we have no insight that such a view pervades our thinking and underpins our motivation and action? What if, in truth, it is not us choosing to be in a union, but the subtleties of a society's influences? What if the same experiment could be repeated to show that like brown eyes were conditioned to believe in their superior status and tall people were to be preferred – marriage bias is also a conditioning?

Let us look at how The Message Bible portrays Paul's views in 1 Corinthians 7:

> *"7. Sometimes I wish everyone were single like me—a simpler life in many ways! But celibacy is not for everyone any more than marriage is. God gives the gift of the single life to some, the gift of the married life to others."*

> *"8-9. I do, though, tell the unmarried and widows that singleness might well be the best thing for them, as it has been for me. But if they can't manage their desires and emotions, they should by all means go ahead and get married. The difficulties of marriage are preferable by far to a sexually tortured life as a single."*

"29-31. I do want to point out, friends, that time is of the essence. There is no time to waste, so don't complicate your lives unnecessarily. Keep it simple—in marriage, grief, joy, whatever. Even in ordinary things—your daily routines of shopping, and so on. Deal as sparingly as possible with the things the world thrusts on you. This world as you see it is on its way out."

"32-35. I want you to live as free of complications as possible. When you're unmarried, you're free to concentrate on simply pleasing the Master. Marriage involves you in all the nuts and bolts of domestic life and in wanting to please your spouse, leading to so many more demands on your attention. The time and energy that married people spend on caring for and nurturing each other, the unmarried can spend in becoming whole and holy instruments of God. I'm trying to be helpful and make it as easy as possible for you, not make things harder. All I want is for you to be able to develop a way of life in which you can spend plenty of time together with the Master without a lot of distractions."

"36-38. If a man has a woman friend to whom he is loyal but never intended to marry, having decided to serve God as a "single," and then changes his mind, deciding he should marry her, he should go ahead and marry. It's no sin; it's not even a "step down" from celibacy, as some say. On the other hand, if a man is comfortable in his decision for a single life in service to God and it's entirely his own conviction and not imposed on him by others, he ought to stick with it. Marriage is spiritually and morally right and not inferior to singleness in any way, although as I

indicated earlier, because of the times we live in, I do have pastoral reasons for encouraging singleness."

If we do not re-examine our desire to leave the single life, we could continue to miss the gift God has for us and never live the John 10: 10 abundant life He has for us. Worse long reflections – don't you think? Singles have the potential to achieve more for the Kingdom of God and its advancement than married couples.

Who are the various types of singles?

- Unmarried
- Widowed
- Divorced
- Separated
- Called by God to be single
- Single due to circumstance
- Single due to chronic illness or severe disability
- Vocational singles like Monks, Nuns & Priests
- Awaiting marriage in the near future

The issues

Consider the various teens and twenties magazines that are read? What are the subject matters that they deal with? Reading a number of those magazines and books, perhaps three or four times per week and the Bible less, is a clear indicator as to which ones are more likely to have the bigger influence on a day to day basis - influencing thoughts and actions. The things that occupy our thinking (cognitions) are the thoughts that will determine our actions. Cognitive Behavioural principles understand that very well. We need to fill our minds with the things of God.

All things are lawful, but not all things are good. Therefore it is not every film at the cinema that we can justify watching – even if the majority attend (Christians and non-Christians alike). It is not every album we should buy, where the words (and the cover) are not conducive to healthy Christian thoughts. It is not every book that we should read. The book, "Fifty Shades Of Grey" is common reading amongst women and has been normalized; yet it is porn and accepted by most as porn.

The proportion of singles in society is rising. Since 2008 over half of the UK population is single. Singleness issues include such things as dating, cohabitation, widowhood and a number of other issues that of course also affect married couples.

Singleness can mean anything from living alone, to living apart due to imprisonment. Defining "singleness" is not easy when seeking to encompass all those issues. Bridget Jones' Diary and Ally McBeal brought more attention to singleness.

The number of adults living with parents is increasing. Single women form a quarter of the adult church. Single men form one tenth. Finding a Christian man to marry is quite a problem for single Christian women.

For every person who views singleness in a positive way, there is another who regards it negatively. For everyone that loves independence, there are others for whom independence is loneliness. Where one single person feels supported by their Church and fulfilled, another feels badly let down. One will see singleness as liberating and the other, as restrictive. One wants children; another does not. One has little desire for sexual activity, while another struggles every day with temptation.

Some believe the Bible encourages singleness and others view the Bible as preferring women to marry. Some believe the Bible advises them to serve God now whilst single and others view their service as more beneficial when they have married. Two can then chase ten thousand.

To measure singleness by the number of unmarried people is not accurate, due to the decline in the number of people marrying and the increase in cohabitation. Between 1998-1999 a quarter of unmarried women aged 16-59 were co-habiting. 39% of that group were aged between 25-29.

Currently 8% of the population thinks that premarital sex is always wrong. Housing, holidays, gymnasiums and such, are all geared up to singles. To some, to be single may simply mean that they are not in a "sexual" relationship. To another, it could simply mean that they are in search of a partner.

Some young people believe that oral sex does not mean a couple "had sex". Only penile-vagina penetration is considered "real sex." There is a very wide divergence of beliefs.

In the 1960's, only 5% of single women lived with a man before marriage. By the 1990's it was about 70%. Many view it as an alternative to marriage, rather than a preparation for marriage. Cohabitation is more likely to lead to a less stable long-term commitment, which is more likely to lead to a break up. Less than 4% of cohabiting couples stay together for 10 years or more. The more often and longer they cohabit, the more likely they are to divorce later on. Study shows they are more likely to be unfaithful to their partners.

Co-habiting couples accumulate less wealth (but this may change as the tax and welfare differences are being brought into line – including for gay couples). Married men earn 10-40% more and are more successful in their careers, particularly when they become fathers. Cohabitants have more health problems and are more likely to suffer from depression. Cohabiting women are more likely to be abused than wives. They are more likely to break up even if they have children.

More than 20% of children are born to cohabiting couples and only about one third will remain with both parents throughout childhood.

Some more statistics

- Single households have tripled in England & Wales between 1971 to 2008.[14]
- By 2020 the number of one-person households will treble to 253.8 million worldwide.[15]
- Marriage rates have fallen to their lowest level since records began.[16]
- Social trends report in 2009 stated that 24% of people below 30 were married. Whereas in 1971, 75% of women married by age 25.[17]
- The number of married couples is at the lowest since 1895 at 237,000 marriages in England & Wales in 2006, down from 471,000 during world War II.[18]
- 1.9 million families consist of a single parent and dependent children.[19]
- 3 million children live in families headed by a lone parent.[20]
- 25% of all families with dependent children are one parent families.[21]
- Women account for 91% of all lone parent with children families.[22]
- There were 3 million opposite sex cohabiting couples in 2013[23]. This figure has doubled in the last 15 years.

- 1.2 million of these families had dependent children.[24] This figure has also doubled over the last 15 years.

In a survey of published research projects on the effect of cohabitation - *Marriage Lite: The Rise of Cohabitation and it's Consequences*, Patricia Morgan found that:

- On average, cohabitations last less than two years before breaking up or converting to marriage.[25]
- Less than four per cent of cohabitations last for 10 years or more.[26]
- Cohabiting influences later marriages.[27] The more often and the longer that men and women cohabit, the more likely they are to divorce later.[28]
- Both men and women in cohabiting relationships are more likely to be unfaithful to their partners than married people.[29]
- Children born to cohabiting parents are more likely to experience a series of disruptions in their family life.[30]

Births outside of marriage

- In 2011, nearly half of all babies in England and Wales were born outside marriage/civil

partnership (47.2 per cent), compared with 46.8 per cent in 2010 and 40.0 percent in 2001[31]. The figure was 8 per cent in 1971.
- In Northern Ireland, 41.9 per cent of babies born in 2011 were born to unmarried parents. [32]
- In Scotland, more than half (51.7 per cent) of all babies born in Scotland in 2012 were born to unmarried parents. [33]

Divorces

- The number of divorces in England and Wales in 2012 was 118,140, an increase of 582 over the 2011 figure.[34]
- The divorce rate has been stable over the last year standing at 10.8 divorcing people per thousand married population. It was from 13.3 per thousand in 2002.[35]
- The most common age at divorce was 40-44 years.[36]
- Overall 42% of marriages will end in divorce.[37]
- The number of marriages dissolved in Northern Ireland in 2011 was 2,343. This a decrease from 2010 when there were 2,600 divorces. [38]
- There were 9,862 divorces in Scotland in 2011; the lowest number of divorces in Scotland since 1979. [39]

Children affected by divorces

- Half of couples (49 percent) divorcing in England and Wales in 2011 had at least one child aged under 16 living in the family.[40]
- There were 100,760 children aged under 16 in families where the parents were divorcing in 2011.[41] That's 1.76 children aged under 16 per divorcing couple.
- Over a fifth (21 per cent) of the children in 2011 were under five and 64 per cent were under 11. [42]

Family breakdown

Children affected by family breakdown are:

- 75 per cent more likely to fail at school.
- 70 per cent more likely to become addicted to drugs.
- 50 per cent more likely to have alcohol abuse problems.
- 40 per cent more likely to have serious debt problems.

Not having sex before marriage is like becoming a vegetarian!

Everything, even other Christian's views (except God and the very, very clear words of the Bible), is seemingly set against achieving abstinence. You set out with determination; you go out with friends socially. Sometimes the menu (in terms of available guys or girls) does not have very much choice! A bit like the vegetarian option on a restaurant menu.

Your friends are doing it, and they ask you to explain why you are not. It's a bit like being asked why you are a vegetarian. It is not because you want to save animals? But you do not always have a very good reason to explain why you don't have sex before marriage – except you know what the Bible has to say. There is so much pressure to go with the flow, like everyone else around you.

The world tells you a lie – that you should enjoy it now and that there is no price to pay. It does not show you the wrecked lives, psychological scars or later relationship problems. Being a virgin is good; it is very good. It is a beautiful, priceless gift which you can give to your future wife or husband. It accords with God's plan for your life and it is something to be absolutely proud of.

Reasons for not being sexually active before marriage

- God said it.
- There will be guilt.
- There is a risk of pregnancy.
- Sexually transmitted disease is grossly underrated and is a serious problem. It is a significant risk.
- Your future spouse has a right for you to be a virgin when they marry you. It is a great gift that you protect for them.
- You do not marry and then face performance anxieties or performance comparisons with a past partner.
- Self-control, as an important lesson learned before marriage, is a very necessary discipline that will have prepared you well for married life. It is a part of character building.
- There is more likely to be mutually satisfying sexual intercourse, where there is no past negative outcomes. It brings greater levels of excitement and long term enjoyment.
- There will be a psychological impact. The two will have become one, when the relationship ends. Some learn to bury the pain. Some learn to cope, but past sexual experiences can remain and reap a toll in future relationships. You cannot join sexually with someone and expect no repercussion. The two having become one, to later tear apart, will bring hurt.

- God made sex and told man to go forth and multiply. Sex is good, but God's plan puts the practice of sex within marriage only.
- Couples who have had premarital sex tend to break up more frequently.
- Men want to marry a virgin (as of course does a woman).
- Women are twice as likely to have sexual relations with another person whilst married. The reason is, a number of their core needs in the marriage are not being met, but it is met by another male outside of the marriage, where it is more difficult to separate love from sex. She searches for love and affection, but he may just want sex. She sacrifices sex to get the appearance of love.

For his own good purposes

In Genesis 1 - we find the fundamental truth, which is essential to the appreciation of singleness and marriage - that God made male and female for **His own good purpose**.

Life is not fair. We do not all get the best start in life to make us secure adults in the transition from childhood. We are shaped and often the things that shape us take our personalities off at a tangent before the real us has even emerged. The brain then hides that inner child deep inside in order to protect it from further pain and eventually, even we can forget our own inner child. Very rarely we get a glimpse of who the real us might have been, but is hidden behind layers and layers of protective things, which takes the form of "masks people wear".

> *God's grace is all sufficient to forgive us of our sins and to cleanse us from all unrighteousness (1 John 1: 9).*

Chapter 5

Singles, Sex, the Bible, Marriage and their issues (2)

Self Pleasuring (Masturbation)

We do need to discuss this issue from the firm foundation that any sexual activity outside of marriage (between a husband and a wife) goes against God's best plan for us and, as such, is a sin.

Masturbation is like a tin of Quality Street. Many people have different types of issues with it and approaches towards it; the same as their approach to a tin of Quality Street. Here are some of those approaches:

- Those who look and decide, "actually I don't really want one".
- Take one and go with the flow as others are doing.
- Not really fussed whether they do or they don't.
- For whom the time of the day is not quite right. If it were earlier, later or a special occasion, they might indulge.
- Take one to save for a later occasion and to enjoy when they feel better able to enjoy it.
- Take one because they are hungry or perhaps are using it for a specific purpose (to alleviate

hunger or even for energy replacement, as a one-off now and then).
- Notice the tin even before I put it on the floor and offer it around. The very sight of the tin attracted their attention.
- Eagerly take one and now live in anticipation of me inviting them to take another.
- No longer 'hear' or 'listen' to all that I am saying, because the tin of chocolates is so enticing and inviting that they are anticipating the occasion for having another one and are even fantasising about which one they might choose next. The taste and images of the content are enticing and can be a distracting preoccupation.
- Eat one after the other and cannot stop themselves. They go on a binge.

Masturbation can be a little like each of the above. There are a variety of ways in which they can be approached, similar to the variety of ways masturbation can be approached and viewed.

If we do not address the issues when we are younger and leave it for a time in the future when our circumstances change, for example when we get married, then compulsiveness can rule and reign for a long time. It becomes entrenched as a habit. When the terrain is right and feelings demand an outlet, the autonomic system will take over and drive repetitious fulfilment.

Self-condemnation will keep many from using their talents, gifting or just volunteering to help out in church life; the enemy likes that very much. Many give up on using their gifting and talents for Christ, because they cannot stop masturbating. They have reservations and guilt about taking communion.

Life will have dealt many things in the past, which will have messed up the Godly expression on your sexuality. Maybe, therefore, you are a "work in progress" in this area of masturbation. During that work, make sure that your light is still shining bright before men that they may see your good work. Do not let masturbation be the hindrance and intimidation that stunts your effectiveness for Christ. The world does not have time to wait for you to overcome masturbation before they benefit from your gifts, talents and abilities.

Do you actually have a desire to stop? Be honest. Is it a 'want' to stop or is it a 'need' to stop? Where does the 'need' to stop come from? Is it your perception that it is wrong and you want to do the right thing? What is your motive for wanting to stop? Is it a right motive? You see, motive for wanting to stop is a large indicator of outcomes.

It needs to be the 'right' thing for you, because you know that Father wants you to stop. That might be because for you, you never learned 'discipline' in your early walk with Christ and giving up masturbation is an area where He might seek to teach you that discipline. This discipline prepares us for a time to come. It has to do with overcoming and, therefore, being ready to move to the next level in our Christian walk. Wrong motive to change will meet problems along the way.

The change process has stages. Those stages are: Precontemplation, Contemplation, Preparing for Change, Action, Maintaining Change and Relapse. Which stage are you really at? If you assume you are at Action, then starting at that stage (when you truly are not ready for action) will prove problematic. You may first of all need to do some work around "motivation to change" to get you to the right stage.

Remember David's first victory over Goliath. It was his years of practicing as a shepherd boy and defending his sheep against wolves, lions and bears, that prepared him for such a moment as that. It had given him the spirit and the skill he needed to take on the Philistine giant. Discipline starts early in life and prepares us for the bigger things.

The question posed is: is masturbation is acceptable for a Christian? In *1 Cor 7: 2-5* Paul urges us to avoid porneia. In the New Testament Greek, the word porneia covers a broad range of sexual sins, including such things as casual sex, adultery, prostitution and homosexuality. Porneia is sex without a life long commitment to another person. As such, it is a violation of God's plan for us. Committing porneia is a sin against one's own body – because it is the body that joins to another and becomes "one flesh". The heart and the mind do not commit to the other person and therefore it is sin.

We need to begin by looking at God's plan when he created sex and its primary purpose. When we acknowledge that primary purpose, then we realise that anything outside of that primary purpose, falls short and we accept less than what God would have for us.

Sex was created by God to prevent loneliness *Gen 2: 18*; sex was created by God before sin entered the world, for Adam, who despite having God was lonely, until woman was created. As soon as woman was created, he had sex with her and they went on to produce children. However, sex is not just for procreation, it is also for pleasure. It binds two flesh into one and a spiritual bonding takes place when sex is at its height.

Self-pleasuring opens us up to a need for increased sensation. Increased sensation or pleasurable feelings, bring with it fantasies. Fantasies lead us into further sin: *Prov 12:11 & 1 Cor 6: 12*. Self-pleasuring can become our master by which we are controlled. The likelihood is that if we self-pleasure or masturbate before marriage, then it is likely to continue even when married. We never master the discipline of "waiting" and so an absent partner for a period of time will cause us to masturbate.

The guilt of overcoming masturbation becomes the stumbling block in our Christian life, rather than the act of masturbation itself. Masturbation can become a substitute for healthy relationships which should lead to a marriage union. We make ourselves vulnerable to compulsive masturbation, just like compulsive eating and other obsessive compulsions, they become problems that need to be addressed with counselling.

Many years ago, much of the teaching to the youth was from people like Joyce Huggett. It showed a pyramid with graduating stages as to what was acceptable and what was not. Believe it or not, we still have words in the Oxford dictionary called petting, heavy petting, under the clothes or over the clothes!

The joke is told of the Father who said to his daughter's boyfriend "you are not allowed to touch her from her neck downwards". The boyfriend cheekily replied, "that's OK sir, I'll stand her on her head!!"

If you were given a bowl full of fruits, some ripe, juicy and looking tasty and others a little brown, very soft and squiggly and almost gone off because they are overripe, which fruit would you chose? We tend to choose the good-looking fruit. Why? Because we like the best. So it is, that God likes the best for us, but we have a choice. We can accept second best, but second best will always hurt us. There is always a price to pay for second best. It might be that we never recognise that we have lived in second best until late in life when we realise that we have never flowed in the full potential that God had for us; certainly not in the John 10: 10 life which he has for us.

When we go down the second best route, we store up problems for the future. The fact is that life is going to throw at us a lot of hard decisions. The way we negotiate around those decisions will determine our future effectiveness. There are life skills we all of us have to learn and develop. Some of us take longer and so God makes us revisit them again at different stages in our lives.

Masturbation is probably a symptom of a deeper need. Not only loneliness, but such things as "attachment" problems, where we avoid getting too close to other people and reject or push away people who get too close. Those things have to do with more deep-seated issues, mostly arising from childhood.

Child abuse is a significant problem in our society and I know this is a delicate subject, but it may be that some have suffered from child abuse in the past and out of that will come many issues, as yet unaddressed. We are products of our families, and the scripts we learned and inherited from our families are those by which we live life, but mostly subconsciously unknowing. In the midst of those sorts of problems, stopping masturbation will feel like a significant obstacle; one that you may not be able to surmount on your own without counselling.

Masturbation rarely remains a long-term habit just for releasing tension. It is solo sex in which solace is found for some of life's issues. A neural pathway is developed in the brain and repeat becomes a must within a matter of time. Stopping is a battle because habit is what developed in the neural pathway. Will power can last for so long, but recognise the pleasure hormones of dopamine, oxytocin and adrenaline which are released into the pleasure side of the brain creating a "lush" feeling, which demands frequent repeat even when willpower says "no more, I must stop".

Masturbation is lush, but be clear, it is for comfort. Over time, it occurs out of habit and demand for repeat and also to get the next fix of the body's self producing hormones of dopamine, oxytocin and adrenaline.

Gen 38: 8-10 is more likely to be a passage that criticised Onan for his lack of willingness to father children for his dead brother's wife, rather than the fact of being seen to masturbate and spilling his seed on the floor, which displeased God. Here are just some issues that make it most unlikely that we will not be able to stop on our own until the underlying causes and drivers are addressed in one way or another:

- Loneliness – this was the first need which God recognised after he had created man, which needed a solution.
- Compulsion/Addiction – it is highly unlikely you will own up to being addicted. Just like an alcoholic or drug-taker needs other people to identify their addiction, the extent of the problem and dependency is mostly underestimated.
- Addiction to pornography: here we need to think about the different magazines that women and men read. It is not the top shelf stuff in the newsagents, it is also the bottom shelf stuff. The distinction between hard and soft porn is not real. So much more of every day reading is porn. The book "Fifty Shades Of Grey" has been normalised for women reading in public without stigma; yet it is well known and acknowledged to be pron. Hard or soft - does it matter? It is still a stimulant.
- Cyber-sex and internet pornography is a particularly serious problem affecting many people; webcams, Skype and FaceTime all bring the visual stimulant into a place of prominence and greater risk taking.
- Attachment issues may be prevalent and manifesting, yet be unknown - without knowledge of such issues driving the way the relationship is experienced. There can be no control until the fact of attachment issues is brought to the consciousness. Counselling help with this is indicated.

Without help in these areas, you will continue to fight a battle, mostly in vain, unless the Holy Spirit does a transformational healing in your life in answer to prayer. Remember how Jesus dealt with the woman at the well in *John 4*, who was living in adultery? He was merciful; he forgave.

Masturbation avoids the one flesh bonding that only God can bring about between a man and a woman. It has no complementary partner. Masturbation turns one's focus inward upon oneself. God did not design sex to be a solitary experience, but to be shared. What is your excuse for remaining single and still masturbating? Is there a contradiction here in your life? Can you masturbate and yet be within God's plan of remaining single? Is it not better to marry than burn with desire?

Do you feel that you only burn with desire from time to time and so that is not really "burning with desire"? If you masturbate, think about having your pleasure met properly within the context of one-man and one-woman union in marriage.

Self-control is not a word that this society likes to hear. It is absolutely necessary for the Christian, who is going to need this discipline throughout life as a child of God. If we do not learn self-control through lack of self-pleasuring, then we will need to revisit it at another point in our live. We cannot miss out any facet of our walk with God. It will revisit us if we desire to go to higher levels with Him. Learn it now. No more "round and round the mulberry bush".

Unfortunately, once sexual desires are aroused and you have been masturbating it is going to be very difficult indeed to reverse what the physiology of the body is requiring you to do. You do need the help of the Holy Spirit to regain an inner purity and self-control.

Have you not learnt well from the many Bible characters whose lives God has intimately unfolded and exposed to us in graphic detail? We can learn about their failings and their frailties in the way they lived their lives, yet look at what they achieved.

They did not rise to their potential until they overcame their frailties. Frailties can be life-long thorns for us to deal with, but in the midst of that, do not let Satan limit your use, effectiveness and ability – which others are waiting for. The Bible is full of characters who rose above their frailties and it is full of characters who did not rise above their frailties and who remained ineffective, yet were full of so much potential.

Remember the rich man who was unwilling to sell all that he had, because he had so many riches? Anything that we put before God is our idol.

Sexual addition, cyber sex and use of the internet, mobile phones and computers are just some of the modern age technologies that have become our "little Gods". If you doubt this, withdraw the mobile phone or computer from a certain individual for just one week and see what happens. We laugh, but for some, their reliance on them is critical to the well being of their lives.

We should not hate our sexual feelings or ask God to take them away from us. We are encouraged not to awaken love until it is ready. We have to take individual responsibility. There is a price to pay. There is a consequence.

This is what C S Lewis wrote in a letter:

> "I know about the despair of overcoming chronic temptation. It is not serious, provided self-offended petulance, annoyance, a break in records, impatience etc don't get the upper hand. No amount of falls will really undo us if we keep on picking ourselves up each time. We shall be very muddy and tattered children by the time we

> reach home. But the
> bathrooms are all ready, the
> towels put out and clean
> clothes in the airing
> cupboard. The only fatal
> thing is to lose one's temper
> and give it up. It is when we
> have noticed the dirt that
> God is most present in us; it
> is the very sign of his
> presence".[43]

Solomon was addicted to sex; some readers are addicted to sex; some are addicted to pornography; some are addicted to masturbation; some have a fantasy/thought life that is not under control. We fan the flames of desire through our choice of films that we watch, at the cinema or on videos, music videos and magazines. In this society, sexual images are readily available, some we cannot easily filter out of our lives, but others we can and should. We are responsible for fanning the embers/flames of desire in the things we open our eyes to and feed our minds with, when we should be turning off the TV, avoiding such films, music or not buying those particular magazines (even the innocent ones). Be clear of your boundaries. Have they been breached, and breached repeatedly, and for too long?

Don't heap hot coals on your head because you masturbate; don't quench your spiritual calling and its affect any more; don't wait to conquer your sexuality before you step into what God has for you or called you to do. You would laugh wouldn't you, at the person that tells someone else that they must give up smoking before they can become a Christian? Yet that is what we do to ourselves. We limit our availability to God to use us because we feel we must conquer this issue before He can use us. I beg to disagree.

Chapter 6

Singles, sex, the Bible, marriage and their issues (3)

"What is it with men and commitment anyway?"

Ladies, let's have a discussion about that question. First of all, may I put to you a theory? Since it is a theory, it is not fully supported by sufficient data or research. The views are those of *Scott M Stanley, of the University of Denver*; his paper attempts to explain a paradox. Why do men seem to resist marriage when they experience greater net benefits from it than women, and yet they are more likely to endorse beliefs that marriage is important?

Let me first mention some statistics and then the theory or hypothesis. In a phone survey (released in 2002) of 2,300 Oklahoma residents who had been divorced, they were asked about the things that led to the divorce. From a list of 10 things, the major contributor for their divorce was "commitment". In particular, "lack of commitment" scored 85% and was the overriding factor. What is commitment?

The theory suggests that there are two components:

- Personal Dedication - refers to how intrinsically committed the partners are to one another. It has four important components; a desire for a future together, a sense of "us" or "we" (or as being part of a team), a high sense of priority

for the relationship and more satisfaction, with sacrificing for the other person.
- Constraints – are the things that might keep couples together when partners would rather leave or because the going gets tough. They are the things that accumulate as relationships grow and make it hard to break up. They include such things as financial considerations, responsibilities for the children, social pressures and lack of foreseeable alternatives. Those constraints can actually have a positive function as a constraint, and cause an individual to put the brakes on making impulsive catastrophic decisions, sometimes in the heat of the moment.

There are two fundamental things that amplify what commitment is about:

- Developing and maintaining a long-term view is crucial for marital success. Commitment brings a long-term perspective that allows partners to weather the storms in marriage.
- Making a choice to give up choices. We have to reach a point where we are willing to give up some things, rather than keep our options open. A little like the monkey with his hand in the jar, trying to take out as much as he can

with his fist full, but not able to do so unless he first lets go of some.

Recognise, however, that those things are at odds with our current culture. We want to keep our choices open and we do not take a long term view about marriage - that it is for life; rather that "the grass might be greener on the other side" if the going gets too tough. After all, why would someone want to give up any choices in life?

There is a difference between men and women in their views about marriage and commitment. Although married men and women may be equally committed and dedicated to the marriage, on average men see the line between marriage and not marrying quite differently to women. Interestingly, in the survey, they found that men actually saw marriage as more desirable or important and would prefer to be married.

What another survey found was that a gap is opening up between young men and young women in US high schools about their attitudes toward marriage. Increasingly, young women think that marriage really does not matter, but high school males mostly agreed that people who marry live happier lives than those who remain single or cohabit. The popular conception is that men have a phobia of commitment, especially of marriage, and women are the ones eager to move relationships toward commitment.

What could explain this discrepancy? Perhaps something about why men won't commit? A theory, and remember it is only a theory, based on beliefs of men in their twenties, is that men report that they enjoy many of the same benefits by cohabiting, rather than marrying. There are few social pressures for them to get married. Mostly, there are none from family, from friends or from the woman's family.

They associate marriage (but not cohabitation) with the possibility of financial loss. They have a fear that in marriage, a woman will want to have children sooner. They are saying essentially, that they are not ready and that they would like to put such changes off as long as they possibly can, until their late twenties. They report that they are not ready for all the responsibility that comes with marriage. Cohabitation without marriage, provides all the desirable benefits of companionship, but without the risks that accompany marriage.

The theory suggests that men are seeking soul mates; and that men see marriage as a final step in a prolonged process of growing up. 94% express this to be the most important feature of what or who they are looking for in a mate. They believe that a soul mate is someone who will take them as they are and not try to change them.

Part of the reason why they were resisting commitment, leading to marriage, is that they were not sure their co-habitee was actually their soul mate for the long term. Until they find their soul mate they are willing to wait, but enjoy the other benefits. They don't want to "settle" for second best in their choice of a marriage partner, although they don't have the same standards for a choice of "live-in girlfriend…"

The implication of what is not being voiced is this: "*I'm happy here for the time being, sleeping with my partner and letting her care for me in various ways, but I am not sure she is really "the one" for me, and I'm biding my time here while I keep looking around or until I decide that she is the one*". Therefore, in the man's mind, even though in a relationship, he may well still see himself as being "on the market".

There will be many women who are equally uncertain about their future with a particular man and therefore also prefer cohabitation. Some may think their male partners are more locked into a future with them than actually is the case. There is a sense for men, that marriage requires a greater level of mutual dedication and responsibility. A wife has earned the right to tell them what they are doing wrong and be able to restrict their activities and behaviours – but only in marriage. Before then, they should not cross the line.

It is arguable, that a major reason that men live approximately eight years longer if they are married (than if they cohabit) is because they are healthier in various ways. That is probably down to the fact that their wives do tell them what to do, in things that would otherwise affect their health. For example, "you need to go to the doctor to get that looked at?" or "don't you think that you are drinking too much?"

Men think that marriage will change them and that being a husband is very different from being a boyfriend or a live-in partner. They believe there is a greater responsibility that comes with the role of husband, than with the role of boyfriend. Women do not have this same sense that they are going to change dramatically when they cross the line of marriage. I throw this out for discussion.

(If you want to read the document in full, you can down load it from www.Smartmarriages.com "What is it with men and commitment anyway?", by Scott M Stanley of the University of Denver (a lecture delivered in 2002 and updated in November 2004) for publication.

Lessons from Samson and the folly of Jephthah's promise.

Let's look at some characters in the Bible who made poor decisions or exercised bad or unwise behaviour. Later we shall look at wise and good behaviours and the rewards.

When we get it wrong with God, it goes badly wrong! Consider the characters of Samson, the folly of Jephthah and the lessons that we can learn because God included their stories in the Bible. We can read about Samson in Judges 13 – 16.

Samson is a sad character and a painful one to read about. Let's look at some things that God promised him and the things God required from him in return. In other words, look at the blessings life holds if we fulfil His promises (see Chapter 14: 24), but the downfall, where we go against God's promises.

Samson was a Nazarite and so he had even extra obligations. We become Christians and have obligations. He failed to comply with his obligations (see Chapter 13: 7 and 14). He gave his heart to Delilah (see Chapter 16:15 and 18). He loved women and he was compulsive in his behaviours. His approach to life was - I see, I desire, I must have, I take. He lacked discipline.

He was not a good judge of people; he was not a good judge of circumstances. He played with fire whilst the Philistines were waiting in the other room to arrest him (see Chapter 16: 9). He was womaniser, he disrespected his parents, he spoke disrespectfully to them, he did not honour them. The promise of long life was no longer to be his portion. If you dishonour your parents, you will have problems honouring God. In fact, to dishonour your parents is to dishonour God.

Samson was unevenly yoked, despite advice from his parents and he will have known of God's commandment to the children of Israel about being unevenly yoked with other nations. He had a bad, bad temper. He touched the dead and their carcasses regularly, which he was forbidden to do. He lusted, wanted sex and took sex, and even went to a prostitute.

He was very foolish, particularly in setting a riddle, being enticed to tell the riddle and sailing close to the wind, sometimes throwing caution to the wind, as he told from where his strength came to him. He was selling his soul, his relationship with God, in a playful, love-enchanted way, that had major repercussions. He sold his spirit cheaply and lightly.

He sinned easily and lightly. He broke his parents' hearts in their later years. Samson's father, Manoah, was not always wise. His wife seemed to exercise more wisdom (see Chapter 13: 22 - 23). Manoah thought that because they had seen the Angel of God that they would die. His wife effectively said to him, "You silly man. Why would God send an Angel to tell us good news, that we are to have a child, and kill us? No, you are wrong". So often it is the wisdom of a woman that is brought to bear in tricky situations.

The signs of Delilah taking his soul, were apparent and yet he would not give her up (see Chapter 16:16). "His soul was vexed to death". He had many warning signs and he ignored them. There is nothing worse than to hear God say that He is against us or for a person not even to know that God's Spirit has left them (see Chapter 16: 20). Often those who befriend us, turn out to be the same ones who turn against us, as happened with the prodigal son.

Before God's Spirit leaves us, we have numerous warning signs, but time and time again we override them. A bit like safety mechanisms put in place to protect us, but we sometimes override them in our preference for haste.

God's voice can then become quieter and quieter and eventually be snuffed out. We begin to rationalise the things we do. We still function and appear to be bearing fruits in our ministry and not know that God's Spirit has left us. That is tragic. Samson never achieved his potential. He could have achieved so much if he had walked hand in hand with God. Will that be said of you?

Do not make unwise promises to God. There is no need to barter with God. He gives us promise (with conditions). It is for us to fulfil the conditions. He has already done His part. The promise is waiting for our condition to be fulfilled and then we can open the gift.

We can see the folly of other characters like Jephthah in Judges 11: 34 - 40. He made a most unwise promise to God that the first person that came out of his home to greet him, he would sacrifice to God. That person was to be his daughter and so she had to be given up.

Three single women in the Bible

Now let us consider three characters in the Bible and the decisions they made and consider the consequences of those decisions. We need to remind ourselves about the story in the Book of Ruth. Here, we see three single women, all three of whom were widows and therefore single. Each made a different choice.

We all have choices. Things may have been done to us in childhood and create a propensity towards us behaving in particular ways, but as adults, we are responsible for our choices and the consequences of poor choices.

The three women had choices as to how they reacted to their respective major traumas. One went her own way and we hear nothing else about her in the Bible. Another accepted her lot in life, but became a conduit to get the third woman to where God had destined and both benefitted greatly. The third woman rose above her adversity and her name is recorded in the annuls of the Bible forever!

Look at the lessons we can learn from Ruth in her journey towards courtship. She had boundaries. A good mother-in-law aided her boundaries. In modern church life we need to pay regard to Titus 2: 3 – 4, which requires church leaders to train older women to be temperate so that in turn they can instruct the younger women.

Ruth was active and not passive, in trying to change her position. She was a stranger in a strange land and all the more reason for her to be timid. She put herself in a place where she could be noticed. She gave God something to use – her availability and willingness to go and do.

She took advice from a trusted advisor and one who cared about her well-being, and offered her best side to the one she wanted to woo. She looked after herself and adorned herself, and continued at all times to be respected by those that looked on and remained within her boundaries.

Others knew of her good reputation. She took heed of "not being unevenly yoked" and words of wisdom from Song of Solomon, encouraging daughters (and indeed males as well) not to awaken love until the right time. She thereby remained faithful and loyal to herself, to her family and to God.

Are there some lessons that you can learn from Ruth? What was her reward? A new man/husband, pleasure, a new home, security, a baby and an inheritance and therefore a future, a helper/carer for her child and the list goes on. Why? Because Matthew 6: 33 does work: "Seek first the kingdom of God and all these things will be added unto you."

God knows that marriage is not easy. That is why He says in *1 Cor 7: 28*, *"... those who marry will face many troubles in this life"* and in the verse before that He says *"... are you loosed from a wife?"* Do not seek a wife (ie do not seek another one!).

What should I be doing in the meantime?

It can feel as if age is not with you and there are time constraints to finding a partner. There are many pressures; one being the pressure to have sex outside of marriage. Hormones are flying all over the place; particularly in the early hours of the morning. Until God answers your prayer for a partner, learn well some lessons now and not keep going around and around the mulberry bush year after year as He tries to get you to see and learn. Learn those lessons now. Apply God's plan.

Here are some promises. You do your part and this is what God will do:

- Like a tree planted by water, you will have your needs met

- You will bear fruit at the right time, not out of season
- You shall be able to stand firm in the face of difficult times and opposition
- What you put your hands to do in God's name will prosper

If you decide not to take up God's promise, then the opposite will be the case. You cannot then rely upon these promises. God has mapped out a course for you, more wonderful than you could come up with on your own. Pertinent questions you need to be considering include "*What is your* motive for being in a relationship? Would you know it if the person of your dreams was right in front of you?" Are you giving up your gift from Him to remain single and maximise your potential, because of the pervasive attitude of a society which may look down on singleness?

Sol 8: 4 urges us not to arouse or awaken love until it so desires. The desires of the flesh want to have sexual contact sooner rather than later. Wisdom within us says wait. Prov 19: 11 says, "*A Man's wisdom gives him patience*". Prov 7: 18 portrays a victim lured into romance and sexual pleasures, as being devoid of responsibility.

A person is made up of body, mind and spirit. We are being prepared and all of those facets need to be developed and be in ongoing preparedness. Therefore there are some skills we need to be developing, whether or not marriage is an aspiration. We need to learn about many things, such as intimacy, which may be "non sexual"; people and developing people skills; how to communicate effectively; how to avoid, manage and reduce conflict; good relationship skills, as a part of equipping us for the future; what love is and what it is not. There is much to do as we wait for His time.

We live in a consumer society, a throwaway society. When something is broken, we no longer want to repair it. There is a throw away mentality and that the grass is greener on the other side. There are no guarantees in relationships.

The pain and the psychological price are not talked about. God does have a perfect plan for our lives. Our role is to find it and implement it. We need to spend time talking to him, and may need to action things that we don't feel good about actioning. We may have to do work in order to "test" our gifting.

God's time is His time. The problem is we want His timing to be our timing. He knows our desire for a partner and he knows the perfect right time. We can try to hasten it, but we know what will happen. It may send us off at a tangent and take many years for us to come back into line with Father and his best plan.

A good marriage does not just happen. There are skills to be learned before then. We need to be equipped. Now is the time to be equipped. When we find ourselves in a compromised position, where we may transgress God's law, we should do as Joseph did and flee, quickly, even if it means leaving our coat behind.

Chapter 7

Sin and iniquity

Observe how these words are actually used quite distinctly in the Bible. For example, in Ps 51: 9 *"Hide Your face from my sins, And blot out all my iniquities"*.

There is a difference between sin and iniquity - see Rom 4: 7 - 8. Exod 34: 7 reminds us that the consequences of sin in the family line spans three or four generations. Deut 23:2 warns us that the consequences of sexual sin lasts even longer.

Sin is to miss the mark. It is transgression, trespass and disobedience. Iniquity is contempt or violation of the law or rebellion; it is crookedness, injustice and perverseness and is a predisposition to sin; to commit the same sin.

We are all affected by the generational iniquity of our ancestors. We are all prone and vulnerable to sin in the same areas as our ancestors. Each generation multiplies the problem for the children following in the family line. Consider Abraham and David's line concerning sexual sin and, in particular, laying with someone forbidden to them. In David's line we see Judah (Jacob's son) lying with Tamar (Judah's own daughter in law). We see David lusting and desiring after Bathsheba and taking her, then committing murder to cover his deeds.

In the same line we see Amnon (David's son) lusting after Tamar (his half sister) and raping her. We see Absalom sleeping with David's concubines. We see Solomon become a sex addict! How many wives and concubines did he have? And they led him astray from following after the Lord and were his downfall.

The Old Testament talked about a scapegoat being sacrificed to break generational sins. See Lev 16:15-16 & 21-22. In the New Testament we then see Jesus paying the price when He died on the cross and became the scapegoat once and for all, for all mankind. The price is paid for you and I, but we need to claim it.

There is a need to break generational iniquities, which become a blight and a curse. Otherwise the predisposition to repeat the same sin will remain. Therapists find it useful to identify how it is that the past can live in the present and how negative behavior patterns repeated generation after generation can have its tentacles into a client's future. A tool is to prepare a genogram (a type of family tree). A genogram can show us patterns and traits that follow down the family line and is very useful in identifying common traits in individuals and families through the generation.

We need to be set free from the inheritance of generational iniquity - John 1: 12 – 13. Rather than repeat the iniquity of a past generation, we need to live under Jer 31: 30: *"...but everyone shall die for his own iniquity..."* Also see Ezek 18: 19 - 20. Grace and mercy is what Jesus offers us.

You can't do better until you know better. You need to know better, so you can do better and fulfil that John 10: 10 promise.

First, let's observe what it can look like when there is disobedience in a bloodline. Observe King Saul's disobedience, which stored up a massive and tragic consequence for his future lineage which affected others. Here is what it looked like:

1 Sam 15: 2 – 3 (NKJV)

2 "Thus says the Lord of hosts: 'I will punish Amalek for what he did to Israel, how he ambushed him on the way when he came up from Egypt.

3 Now go and attack Amalek, and utterly destroy all that they have, and do not spare them. But kill both man and woman, infant and nursing child, ox and sheep, camel and donkey.'"

Here is what Saul did. 1 Sam 15: 7 – 9 (NKJV)

7 "And Saul attacked the Amalekites, from Havilah all the way to Shur, which is east of Egypt.

8 He also took Agag king of the Amalekites alive, and utterly destroyed all the people with the edge of the sword.

9 But Saul and the people spared Agag and the best of the sheep, the oxen, the fatlings, the lambs, and all that was good, and were unwilling to utterly destroy them. But everything despised and worthless, that they utterly destroyed."

This is God's response through Samuel the prophet. 1 Sam 15: 13 – 21 (NKJV)

13 Then Samuel went to Saul, and Saul said to him, "Blessed are you of the Lord! I have performed the commandment of the Lord."

14 But Samuel said, "What then is this bleating of the sheep in my ears, and the lowing of the oxen which I hear?"

15 And Saul said, "They have brought them from the Amalekites; for the people spared the best of the sheep and the oxen, to sacrifice to the Lord your God; and the rest we have utterly destroyed."

16 Then Samuel said to Saul, "Be quiet! And I will tell you what the Lord said to me last night."

And he said to him, "Speak on."

***17** So Samuel said, "When you were little in your own eyes, were you not head of the tribes of Israel? And did not the Lord anoint you king over Israel?*

***18** Now the Lord sent you on a mission, and said, 'Go, and utterly destroy the sinners, the Amalekites, and fight against them until they are consumed.'*

***19** Why then did you not obey the voice of the Lord? Why did you swoop down on the spoil, and do evil in the sight of the Lord?"*

***20** And Saul said to Samuel, "But I have obeyed the voice of the Lord, and gone on the mission on which the Lord sent me, and brought back Agag king of Amalek; I have utterly destroyed the Amalekites.*

***21** But the people took of the plunder, sheep and oxen, the best of the things which should have been utterly destroyed, to sacrifice to the Lord your God in Gilgal."*

Observe the consequences of Saul's disobedience. It led to loss of his life, but not in a way to be expected. A battle with Israel's arch enemy is raging.

1 Sam 31: 1 – 5 (NKJV)

***1** "Now the Philistines fought against Israel; and the men of Israel fled from before the Philistines, and fell slain on Mount Gilboa.*

2 Then the Philistines followed hard after Saul and his sons. And the Philistines killed Jonathan, Abinadab, and Malchishua, Saul's sons.

3 The battle became fierce against Saul. The archers hit him, and he was severely wounded by the archers.

4 Then Saul said to his armor bearer, "Draw your sword, and thrust me through with it, lest these uncircumcised men come and thrust me through and abuse me." But his armor bearer would not, for he was greatly afraid. Therefore Saul took a sword and fell on it.

5 And when his armor bearer saw that Saul was dead, he also fell on his sword, and died with him".

But Saul was not yet in fact dead. Observe the ironic twist to Saul's end.

2 Sam 1: 1 – 10 (NKJV)

1 Now it came to pass after the death of Saul, when David had returned from the slaughter of the Amalekites, and David had stayed two days in Ziklag,

2 on the third day, behold, it happened that a man came from Saul's camp with his clothes torn and dust on his head. So it was, when he came to David, that he fell to the ground and prostrated himself.

3 And David said to him, "Where have you come from?"

So he said to him, "I have escaped from the camp of Israel."

4 Then David said to him, "How did the matter go? Please tell me."

And he answered, "The people have fled from the battle, many of the people are fallen and dead, and Saul and Jonathan his son are dead also."

5 So David said to the young man who told him, "How do you know that Saul and Jonathan his son are dead?"

6 Then the young man who told him said, "As I happened by chance to be on Mount Gilboa, there was Saul, leaning on his spear; and indeed the chariots and horsemen followed hard after him.

7 Now when he looked behind him, he saw me and called to me. And I answered, 'Here I am.'

*8 And he said to me, 'Who are you?' So I answered him, '**I am an Amalekite**.'*

9 He said to me again, 'Please stand over me and kill me, for anguish has come upon me, but my life still remains in me.'

10 So I stood over him and killed him, because I was sure that he could not live after he had fallen. And I took the crown that was on his head and the bracelet that was on his arm, and have brought them here to my lord."

An Amalekite actually killed Saul. Look at 1 Chron 10: 13 (NKJV)

13 So Saul died for his unfaithfulness which he had committed against the Lord, because he did not keep the word of the Lord, and also because he consulted a medium for guidance.

Saul's family also paid a price for his disobedience, since he passed on his iniquity. Ishbosheth was Saul's son and he did come to the throne of Israel after Saul – (2 Sam 2: 10). He was, however, soon murdered – (2 Sam 4: 5 – 7). Saul's grandson (by Jonathan) was called Mephibosheth and he was crippled in his feet – (2 Sam 4: 4). Mephibosheth ended up in Lo Debar ("a place of nothing") – 2 Sam 9: 5 – 6), until David brought him out.

There is an ambiguity as to whether Mephibosheth was ultimately entirely faithful – (2 Sam 19: 24 – 30).

Enter the stage Esther, some 500 years later when the children of Israel were now in exile in a foreign land - Esther 3: 1:

3 "After these things King Ahasuerus promoted Haman, the son of Hammedatha the Agagite, and advanced him and set his seat above all the princes who were with him".

An Agagite is a descendant of Agag King of the Amalekites – a people that should have been utterly destroyed by King Saul. If Saul had obeyed the command of the Lord, then Esther would not have needed to enter Israel's history. A merciful God provided yet another way out – another saviour for His people. Merciful God.

Look again at the folly of the Children of Israel in what may be called the Gibeonite Principles. In Joshua 9: 3 - 4 the Gibeonites may have acted craftily to deceive the Israelites and cause them to make a treaty with them, but what they did recognise was that their past did not guarantee their future safety. To their credit, they acted.

Don't try to turn them into your servants or think that you can domesticate and tame your past habits, mistakes and behaviours. They will bite you in the bum when things seem to be going well and you least expect it. Don't make pacts with your enemy.

The grace of God is unmerited love and unmerited favour

So then, what is Grace? Grace is God's unmerited favour. This what we read in Titus 2:11-12 Amplified Bible (AMP):

11 For the grace of God (His unmerited favor and blessing) has come forward (appeared) for the deliverance from sin and the eternal salvation for all mankind.

12 It has trained us to reject and renounce all ungodliness (irreligion) and worldly (passionate) desires, to live discreet (temperate, self-controlled), upright, devout (spiritually whole) lives in this present world.

The grace of God is unmerited love and unmerited favour. But it is also an empowerment and enablement. We often tolerate sin because we know the grace of God is available. When we miss the mark, the grace of God is available to forgive us, but we are empowered not to sin in the first place and to overcome sin. Not just to tolerate it. We often use the phrase *"I am human"* to justify failings.

Grace is God's strength to overcome our shortcomings with confidence. Verse 12 tells us that grace also teaches us. It teaches us to deny ungodly and worldly lusts so we can live soberly, righteously and godly in this present world. He has taught/enabled/empowered/given us the grace to overcome.

We need to put on His grace as we listen, resolve and determine to apply the things we hear and are taught. Our willpower will fail, but His empowerment is what will enable us to succeed and not keep on missing the mark.

Remember Isaiah 5: 13 Amplified Bible (AMP):

13 Therefore, My people go into captivity [to their enemies] without knowing it and because they have no knowledge [of God]. And their honorable men [their glory] are famished, and their common people are parched with thirst.

The verse refers to Christians and not to the unsaved. Scary stuff when we do not even realise that we are in captivity. We go into captivity in our minds and our actions then support what our mind is dwelling on. Remind yourself that Fear is to meditate on the wrong thing.

Many of us are captives because we deny the knowledge of God's grace. That grace is power that we need in this life as humans.

That, which an earlier generation of a family did, can have reprisals on a future line in that families generation. Positives breeds positives. Negatives breed negatives.

You are cut off from His provision for you and kept from experiencing the John 10: 10 abundance because of lack of knowledge. We remain in lack and bondage because of what we don't know. Prov 4: 7 *"And in all your getting, get understanding"*.

GRACE = NOW NO CONDEMNATION

The very nature of Christ Jesus is inside of you when you are born again. You are empowered. Stop denying the authority, grace and power that you have. You deny it because of your lack of knowledge and lack of use.

The bottom line is this – *"Where sin abounded, Grace abounded much more"* – Roms 5: 20. Think on these things throughout the day.

Resolve to take up the nature of Christ in your living of life.

What is God's answer to sin and iniquity?

When we pray and ask for forgiveness from the heart, God does hear and does blot out our sin, as far as the east is from the west. Let's, however, look at iniquity and God's covenant of Mercy.

Just like iniquity can be passed down the generational line, so can a covenant of mercy from the Lord and that will cancel out iniquities and instead bless the lineage of future generations. This is what it looked like for King David in 2 Sam 7: 1-16:

2 Samuel 7:12-16 (NKJV)

12 "When your days are fulfilled and you rest with your fathers, I will set up your seed after you, who will come from your body, and I will establish his kingdom.

13 He shall build a house for My name, and I will establish the throne of his kingdom forever.

14 I will be his Father, and he shall be My son. If he commits iniquity, I will chasten him with the rod of men and with the blows of the sons of men.

15 But My mercy shall not depart from him, as I took it from Saul, whom I removed from before you.

16 And your house and your kingdom shall be established forever before you. Your throne shall be established forever."

Iniquity gets passed on to the third and fourth generations, but know for sure that a covenant of mercy is passed on for an even longer period – a thousand generations. That is cause for real excitement and praise! Read it in Deut 7: 9:

Deuteronomy 7:9 (NKJV)

9 "Therefore know that the Lord your God, He is God, the faithful God who keeps covenant and mercy for a thousand generations with those who love Him and keep His commandments;

Therefore, after David's death, Solomon his son, benefits from God's covenant of mercy with David and we read in 1 Kings11: 6 – 13:

6 "Solomon did evil in the sight of the Lord, and did not fully follow the Lord, as did his father David…

11 Therefore the Lord said to Solomon, "Because you have done this, and have not kept My covenant and My statutes, which I have commanded you, I will surely tear the kingdom away from you and give it to your servant.

12 Nevertheless I will not do it in your days, for the sake of your father David; I will tear it out of the hand of your son.

13 However I will not tear away the whole kingdom; I will give one tribe to your son for the sake of My servant David, and for the sake of Jerusalem which I have chosen."

See also 1 Kings 11: 29 – 32:

29 "Now it happened at that time, when Jeroboam went out of Jerusalem, that the prophet Ahijah the Shilonite met him on the way; and he had clothed himself with a new garment, and the two were alone in the field.

30 Then Ahijah took hold of the new garment that was on him, and tore it into twelve pieces.

31 And he said to Jeroboam, "Take for yourself ten pieces, for thus says the Lord, the God of Israel: 'Behold, I will tear the kingdom out of the hand of Solomon and will give ten tribes to you

32 (but he shall have one tribe for the sake of My servant David, and for the sake of Jerusalem, the city which I have chosen out of all the tribes of Israel)…"

Look also at 2 Kings 19: 32 – 34: Some 305 years after David's death. Hezekiah is now on the throne of Judah and is a descendent of David.

2 Kings 19:32-34

32 "Therefore thus says the Lord concerning the king of Assyria: 'He shall not come into this city, nor shoot an arrow there, nor come before it with shield, nor build a siege mound against it.

33 By the way that he came, by the same shall he return; and he shall not come into this city,' says the Lord.

34 'For I will defend this city, to save it . For My own sake and for My servant David's sake.'"

Also see 2 Kings: 35 – 36:

35 And it came to pass on a certain night that the angel of the Lord went out, and killed in the camp of the Assyrians one hundred and eighty-five thousand; and when people arose early in the morning, there were the corpses—all dead.

36 So Sennacherib king of Assyria departed and went away, returned home, and remained at Nineveh.

What an awesome God we serve. Smile and rejoice, with praise at the potential of your inheritance. Seek a covenant of mercy with your God. It is our act of obedience to God, His will and His purpose for your life that creates that covenant of mercy. Have an earnest desire on your part to please him with a legacy of faith, which God can use to honour your generations. Your faith and obedience builds an account of mercy that you can redeem. That is by far, the best legacy you can leave as a gift to your children, their children's, children's, children's children....

We are given a second, third, fourth and repeated opportunity to get it right with God. His mercy is unfailing, but it cost. It cost God His son – Jesus Christ. Thank you Father for not giving up on ME.

You can repeat these words: "*No more to sin and iniquity. I repent and reject sin in my life. Because of the Blood of Jesus Christ, I break sin and iniquity for good. In Jesus' name, Amen*".

You may have unfinished business to complete between you and God after reading this chapter. Get on and do it now. Do it and seal your future.

The blessings you deposit will always earn interest and multiply. The blessings overcome the curse. He whom God blesses cannot be cursed.

Leave a legacy in your family line which breaks generational iniquities and replaces them with the blessings which flow from a covenant of mercy – which flows for a thousand generations.

Here is a prayer for being set free from generational sin caused by iniquity:

"Thank you Lord Jesus, that you have rescued me from the kingdom of darkness and brought me into the kingdom of light. You have redeemed me with your precious blood and I belong to you. I have been born again and I am a member of the family of God. Jesus is Lord.

I am also a member of the human family. I identify with them and confess that we have sinned and broken your laws. We have done this in thought, word and deed and in particular by involvement in [be specific about the matter].

I forgive my ancestors for the consequences of their sins that have affected me. I take responsibility for the ways in which I have repeated their sins and I repent of my sin. Please forgive me. I pray this in Jesus' name. Amen."

Here is a prayer to receive cleansing from the consequences of generational iniquity:

"In the name of Jesus I confess, renounce and revoke every curse, vow, oath, decision, choice, contract and covenant made by my forebears (and by myself) in agreement with the will of Satan and the powers of darkness, at any time, in any place, with any person and any purpose. I choose today to come in line with the will of God, under the new covenant of the precious blood of Jesus, which cleanses me from all sin.

Appropriating what Jesus bought for me on the cross of Calvary, I take the sword of the spirit and cut off all generational links – in His mighty name. Thank you that I am now parented by Father God. I am His child. I thank you Jesus that you bear all the iniquity in my life and I therefore claim freedom from all curses, heredity diseases and other consequences of the sins of my forebears. I ask it in Jesus' name. Amen."

Chapter 8

Belief theories in Cognitive Behavioural Therapy (CBT)

The mind is part of the soul

A person is made up of body, mind and spirit. We are being prepared and all of those facets need to be developed and be in ongoing preparedness. Therefore, there are some skills we need to be developing, whether or not marriage is an aspiration.

We need to learn about such things as intimacy, which may be "non sexual". We need to learn about people and gain people skills. We need to learn how to communicate effectively. We need to learn how to avoid, manage and reduce conflict. We need to learn good relationship skills, as a part of equipping us for the future. We need to learn what love is and what it is not.

The soul is made up of the mind, emotions and the will. Changing the mind is an ongoing process. It is about "renewing" the mind and needs a conscious effort and action. It is not spontaneous when we are born again. Romans 12:2 – *"...and do not be conformed to this world, but be transformed by the renewing of your mind"*. God invented CBT and CBT principles long before man stumbled upon them!

After becoming a Christian, we will remain conformed to the world until our mind is renewed. We may be headed to heaven, but whilst here on the earth we may not be experiencing that promised abundant life.

When our mind is truly renewed by the Word of God, we will overcome negative desires. In Romans 12:2 the word "transformed" means to go through a complete change in form or kind, in the same way as we see a caterpillar change from cocoon to a butterfly during the metamorphosis process.

Renewing the mind is not a one-time occurrence; it is a constant labour and effort of repeated practice. It needs to become a lifestyle and not remain a one time experience.

Strongholds are thoughts and attitudes that have such a grip on our mind that they affect and control our thinking. We can bring our thought processes under our authority and make them captive to the Word of God. The enemy's role is to sabotage those endeavours.

The underlying theory behind CBT suggests that we have three levels of cognitions/thinking. They are core beliefs, intermediate beliefs and automatic thoughts.

- Core beliefs: this is the most fundamental level of belief. It is global, very rigid and over generalised. For example, *"I am a useless. No-one likes or trusts me. Everything gets messed up when*

I become involved". The person may not always be consciously aware of the belief that they hold about themselves and that they, in fact, hold them as absolute truths - even though sometimes said in jest.

- Intermediate beliefs: these are sets of attitudes, rules and assumptions that come out of the influences of the core beliefs above. For example, if I come second, it shows I am a failure. If I win anything, there must be something wrong with the prize. We are not always consciously aware of these beliefs.
- Automatic thoughts: these are generated in given situations and stem out of the core belief and intermediate beliefs. This is as conscious as the awareness will get. For example, I must not do this. It is wrong.

Let us examine each of these in more detail. Past experiences have an effect on how we think and function. Bad experiences may have been endured and gotten over, but frequently they leave unpleasant events and a mark, not just in the present but also affect the future.

There are some tools enabling us to examine the effects of past experiences and how they might have led to us developing core beliefs that may be causing current emotional difficulties and behaviours. CBT does not focus intensively on childhood relationships and experiences, but also investigates how those past experiences may be affecting the present life.

The past can influence the present in a very significant way. Growing up with parents who fought a lot may have taught us to be very quiet and keep out of the way at those times so that any anger is not directed at us. We may have had critical parents who made high academic demands, frequently interpreted as love and approval only when high achievements were attained. Not being able to predict the mood of a parent, who at times could be very violent when in a bad mood and at other times very loving and funny, may have left a legacy.

Unfaithful partners causing frequent relationship breakups may also cause insecurity and high levels of suspicion in current relationships. Loss of a business, loss of a partner, death of a child, depression, teenage pregnancy can all paint a picture of being dogged with bad luck.

In all of these situations, we can develop negative core beliefs that have a profound effect on our mental health. That contributes to the way that we think about other people, the world and ourselves.

Core beliefs are enduring ideas or core philosophies, which we hold very strongly and very deeply. They are not always negative. Good experiences generally lead to healthy ideas about ourselves, other people and the world. However, it is the negative core beliefs that we concentrate upon. Core beliefs tend to be global and absolute and held to 100%, under all conditions. They are often formed from childhood experiences and so never fully evaluated. They help the child to make sense of the adult world and experiences. We may, however, continue to act, think and feel that way in adulthood. They are very central to our belief system.

Those core beliefs give rise to rules, demands, and assumptions that produce the automatic thoughts. Those automatic thoughts just pop into our head when we are confronted with a situation. Issues may arise from predisposing factors and precipitants, and maintaining factors.

The core beliefs are so strong that they are used as lens or filters, through which we interpret all the information we receive from other people and the world around us. Identifying your core beliefs can help you to understand why you keep having the same problems.

If core beliefs are held deeply, we may not think of them or actually hear them in our own head as the clear statements that they are. It is probably more likely that we are more in tune with the negative automatic thoughts that arise out of the core beliefs.

Turning unhealthy and absolute core beliefs into alternatives is not about positive thinking, but it is about loosening our rigidity of thoughts and feelings and generating less absolute and more accurate, more realistic opinions about ourselves, other people and the world around us.

Let us also look at the values that we hold. Our values are rigid such that they are not easily changed or given up. They are caught not taught.

It is not a matter of changing our core beliefs or values or even giving them up; it is about recognising the things that go on in our lives and affect us, many of which we have no conscious knowledge about. We are moving some things from the unconscious to the conscious. When we understand this much better, then we can start to examine what are our core beliefs and better understand how they can be working away in the unconscious.

Reclaiming your life

I wonder whether, more accurately, we should be talking about claiming your life for the first time, rather than reclaiming something you never did have in the first place. Early childhood influences and adversities could have caused the infant's personality to be shaped very differently from the unique and potentially very different individual that could have blossomed. Therefore the real personality never did evolve.

Our beliefs can be the very thing that stop us achieving desired change. Challenging our beliefs (cognitions) by supplying new information on which to base new learning can affect change. Challenging the evidence for a particular belief may show the belief to have no proper foundation and result in revised thinking. That is called cognitive restructuring. Cognitive restructuring (by challenging a particular belief) alongside behavioural change can be more effective in creating change.

There are unconscious factors that keep repetitive negative behaviour and practices in place. Lack of knowledge of them means you are destined to keep on repeating them. Here are the three factors:

- Predisposing factors: these are some general upbringing experiences (from childhood), which includes cultural, social, religious norms and the attitudes and beliefs those experiences create. Each of us have particular personality traits that make us less or more vulnerable to the influence of adapting past negative behaviour traits into our present, which then affects our future. A particular behaviour practiced repeatedly in childhood can predispose us (set down a script in our minds) that cause us to continue to behave in that

particular way into adulthood. The behaviour predisposes us to behave in that way.
- Precipitating factors: There may be experiences, events or expectations that have left a negative impression upon us. They leave a lasting image and impression such that when the scenario is again faced in the future, the brain has an anticipated expectation of another repeated negative outcome even before the activity is undertaken. (Ie a self-fulfilling prophecy of anticipatory failure).
- Maintaining factors: The consequences of a particular behaviour may mean that the behaviour is more likely to be repeated. It is maintained because of habit and repetition.

We have all learned inappropriate pairings and associations that have predisposed us, precipitated and caused us to maintain certain types of behaviours. If we can learn more about those predisposing, precipitating and maintaining factors, we are someway towards changing our cognition. As we change our cognition (the way we think, feel and believe), then we start to change our behaviour. In other words, as we change our mind (our cognition) we can change our life (because we start to change our behaviours as well). What we think is who we are. Where the mind is, the heart will follow. Changing what the mind thinks will also change what the heart follows.

Recognise that if a stimuli has been present for a long time and a behaviour follows, constant repetition means reinforcement has been taking place over the years and habit has set in. Habit is not just something we do. It is based on a stimulus that creates automatic thoughts, beliefs, feelings and then behaviours.

What we do know is that if removing a stimulus from an existing behaviour, so as to extinguish that behaviour, is accompanied by adding a stimulus to a more desired behaviour (with the intention of positive reinforcing it), then extinction of the less desirable behaviour is likely to happen faster.

In CBT, the focus wherever possible is actually to ignore the old behaviour. By ignoring it, you are removing all stimulus that kept the behaviour going, with the intention of extinguishing that old behaviour. At the same time/simultaneously – a new focus of thought, feeling, belief and behaviour in another direction, will positively reinforce a new behaviour. The old and the new will have difficulties continuing side by side. One must get less as the other gets more.

An important principle of learning is that in order to achieve behavioural change, the desired behaviour needs to be broken down into small manageable steps. It is achievement of success at each small manageable step that acts as a positive reinforcer to go on and continue to the next step. Therefore, the new thoughts and behaviours have to be designed in a way that they are undertaken in small manageable steps. Frequently, failure is because the step undertaken to change a behaviour was too large.

Motivation to Change: Stages of Change

Change interventions are sometimes necessary in life to address lifestyle modifications, aimed at preventing further issues. Motivation often focuses on the person's failure and why they failed the last time. Understanding a person's readiness to make change, appreciating the barriers to change and helping individuals anticipate relapse, can better improve outcomes and reduce frustrations.

The stages of change show that, for most people, change in behaviour occurs gradually. A person moves from being uninterested, unaware or unwilling to make a change (pre contemplation), to considering change (contemplation), to deciding and preparing to make a change.

Genuine determined action is then taken. Over time, attempts to maintain the new behaviour occur. Relapses are almost inevitable and relapse actually becomes part of the process of working towards life-long change.

We can see a parallel with where David was at during a stage in preparation to succeed to the throne as the second King of Israel. He had not yet come into the height of his season and purpose for which God had birthed him.

David would not have had to fight a particular fight if history's past had not thrown up an enemy that should not have remained. Saul had been told specifically to utterly destroy the Amalekites. He failed to do so and they now become a source of frustration to David. Years later, and allied with the Philistines in a fight against Israel, David is sent away by the princes of the Philistines. David is in a compromised place. He is in no man's land, between two enemies, trying to do the best that he can do.

He and his men return to the land of the Philistines to find that they had been invaded and their children, wives, animals and goods taken away by the Amalekites. Another enemy has come into their camp and stolen what belongs to David and his men. They were greatly distressed.

This was not a good day for David. He and his men lifted up their voices and wept until they no longer had the power to weep. After weeping, accusations start; allocation of blame and fault. His own men speak of stoning him, which was very distressing. Yet in the midst of this deep despair, David had it within himself to look to his God and strengthen himself in the Lord. He was able to take his eyes off the circumstance and predicament confronting him and look to his God.

He sought God, received his answer and went forward with confidence, belief and assurance that he would regain all that was taken. There was enough recovered to share with his neighbours.

Change: The power of self-control - mastering mindsets

We live with and accept a lower quality of living and can become accepting and comfortable with our status quo and overlook the fact that we do live and function below our full potential. Many people die not having fulfilled their full potential and lived the John 10:10 life which Father said we could have because Jesus paid for it.

John 10:10 (AMP): The second part of the verse says *"...I came that they may have and enjoy life, and have it in abundance (to the full, till it overflows)."*

Many of us, however, omit or overlook the first part of the verse which says *"The thief comes only in order to steal and kill and destroy."*

In the very same verse we see two opposing powers at work: the enemy (Satan) and Jesus. Satan is a pretender; he roars like a lion, but he is not the real thing. There is only one lion: Jesus is the Lion of Judah. He is the only one worthy of our praise and worship.

Problem: most of us have no concept of what the John 10: 10 life is like because we have settled in the land of mediocrity. We have been there for far too long and it is time to come out of the land of Lo Debar. A land and place of "nothing".

But first things first: we have to do what Matt 6: 33 says:

*33 But seek (aim at and strive after) **first** of all His kingdom and His righteousness (His way of doing and being right), and then all these things taken together will be given you besides.*

What we have are promises with conditions. Conditions, but with promises. Promises, but there are conditions. Conditions, but what wonderful promises. Promises and conditions. Promises, but conditions. Understand this well.

Fulfil your part - the conditions - and no - it is not that He will then fulfil His promise. He has already fulfilled His part - the promises. They are signed off, sealed and ready to flow into your life as soon as you fulfil your conditions. Do not attribute slowness to God in fulfilling His promises - His part.

Your past will disguise itself as your friend and ally. Don't settle in Elim where the springs of water will only feed you for a season.

There comes a point when you must cut ties with your past. It may hurt. When you have been living in a compromised place for a long time, by trying to accommodate your past, then attempts at change will see your familiar past turn on you. It will want to maintain its hold in your present and into your future.

This teaching is your invitation to come out of Lo Debar. It is time to come out and up - 2 Sam 9: 4-5. Lo debar means "Nothing" – Amos 6: 13.

See your future first of all. If you can't see it then you cannot claim it or head towards it. See your future and head towards it. It is a journey. It is a walk. Is 28: 10 *"precept upon precept, line upon line, here a little, there a little. It is a journey made up of little incremental steps. Step by step – little by little – bit by bit"*.

If you cannot see a new you in the natural realm, you will never be able to move forward and be able to see **you** in the spiritual realm. You need to renew your mind.

Excuses not to change are usual. An excuse is an enemy to change. Excuses are the nails that are used to build a house of failure. Changed thinking leads to changed feelings, leads to changed action, leads to changed life.

Knowledge alone is not power. Knowledge has value only in the hands of someone who has the ability to think well. We need to learn to think well. When we learn to think well, we can achieve dreams and reach our full potential.

Prov 23: 7   "As people think in their heart so they are."

If your thinking is poor, then you have placed a lid (a ceiling) on your life and your ability to achieve and attain. Where your thinking is limited, so your potential is never allowed to attain higher heights.

A change of thinking can help you move from survival or maintaining the status quo, to real progress.

95% of achieving is knowing what you want and a willingness to pay the price to get it. (Not just a willingness to pay the price - but actually then paying the price). You need to have belief. A belief is not just an idea, but something that holds great power and the ability to change expectations.

People are more willing to embrace change when:

- They hurt enough such that they are at a point of willingness to change.

- They learn enough (through education and knowledge) that they now want to change.
- They receive enough information and they are able to change.

Achievement comes from the habit of good thinking. The more good thinking, the more good thoughts you will continue to think. Good thinking needs to become a good habit. That is a healthy habit.

Every person has the potential to become a good thinker. Unsuccessful people focus their thinking on survival; average people focus their thinking on maintenance; successful people focus their thinking on progress.

Choices turn into action when we first make a conscious "resolve" to do something. We need to arm ourselves with the mind of Christ. We do that by lining up our thinking with His teaching.

Chapter 9

The change process: you too can change your mind in order to change your life

What does sex addiction and love addiction therapy entail? Change.

Change - by overcoming Sex or Love Addiction is an incremental process based on gradual stages. This poem *"Autobiography in Five Chapters"*[44] by Portia Nelson sums it up very aptly:

ONE

As I walk down the street,

There is a deep hole in the side walk.

I fall in.

I am lost...I am hopeless.

It takes forever to find a way out.

TWO

I walk down the same street.

There is a deep hole in the sidewalk.

I pretend I don't see it.

I fall in again.

I can't believe I'm in the same place.

But it isn't my fault

It still takes a long time to get out.

THREE

I walk down the same street.

There is a deep hole in the sidewalk.

I see it is there.

I still fall in…it's a habit.

My eyes are open.

I know where I am.

It is MY fault.

I get out immediately.

FOUR

I walk down the same street.

There is a deep hole in the sidewalk.

I walk round it.

FIVE

I walk down another street…

What you cannot see, you have no chance of affecting or changing. That is because it is working away in the unconscious and is a part of you. It is habit. It does not need to engage the brain or thought power in order to activate the behaviour.

When you can see, you have a chance of beginning to try to affect and change. That is because you have moved it from the unconscious to the conscious and you can now see your behaviour. Seeing it does not mean that you can straight away do anything about it, let alone change it. Habit is entrenched and will take a period of conscious recognition before change can take place over time. Remember the poem by Portia Nelson above. The fact that you walk down the street and can now see the pothole does not me you can instantly avoid it.

Cognitive Behavioural Principles (CBT)

Cognitive behavioural therapy is one of the features of the work used by many sex therapists. It is about what a person actually does (their actions), as well as their thoughts, feelings and beliefs about those behaviours. The thoughts, beliefs and feelings are the cognitions.

The way in which humans learn and adapt their behaviour is a source of constant investigation. Observing animal behaviour has been insightful as to how they learn from habit and repetition. Whilst habit is a constant companion, when we speak about it, we tend to do so with negative connotations. In other words, habit tends to be viewed as negative. In fact, habit comes to our aid every day of our waking life. Without them, the brain might overload as it tries to act out our requirements. Think about the journey to church. Think about the journey to work. So frequently when we look back we realise we went through the traffic lights when they were green and stopped when red. If we walked, we probably took a familiar route. We did not need to concentrate on the route. Our body and brain just took us there. Habit can therefore be helpful. There are, however, some habits that we recognise to be unhelpful and even quite destructive.

Concentrating on behaviour alone can be successful. In other words, concentrating on changing behaviour is helpful. What we know, however, is that taking thoughts and feelings (cognitions) into account, alongside behaviour, can be even more beneficial.

Our belief can be the very thing that stops us achieving desired change. Challenging our beliefs (cognitions), by supplying new information on which to base new learning, can effect change.

Challenging the evidence for a particular belief may show the belief to have no proper foundation and result in revised thinking. That is called cognitive restructuring.

Cognitive restructuring (by challenging a particular belief) alongside behavioural change can be more effective in allowing change and breaking free from negative habits and behaviours which are not having the desired beneficial outcomes – such as in the area of sex.

There are three psychological factors which are significant contributors to sexual problems.

We have already looked at them above in relation to sexual issues. They are predisposing, precipitating and maintaining factors. Let us view them again, but in a wider context, as follows:

- Predisposing factors: there are some general upbringing experiences (from childhood), which includes cultural, social, religious norms, attitudes and beliefs which our experiences create that leave a legacy for the future. Certain behaviours observed as a child can predispose (set down a script in our minds) that cause us to behave in that particular way. In other words, the behaviour predisposes them to behave in that way in the future.

Example: When we were young and our parents turned off the television whenever there was a couple becoming amorous, that may have left us with an impression that there is something embarrassing about kissing and sex. The nature of the brain is to become inquisitive about the secrecy behind the actions of our parents.

- Precipitating factors: there may be experiences, events or expectations that we have and hold to even before a particular behaviour is displayed. When a particular behaviour, from others, manifest themselves, they may trigger a reaction to behave and respond in a prescribed way.

Example: The smell of alcohol may have created a sense of agitation anxiety and that flows from past experiences an alcoholic father causing grief for the whole household when drunk. Repeating a sexual scenario – which has a legacy of failure – means that when that scene is again before us, it has set up a precipitant or anticipatory failure is again inevitable.

- Maintaining factors: The consequences of repetitive negative outcomes from patterns of behaviour may mean there is an expectation of the same negative outcome on each occasion in the future. Therefore the consequences are expected and maintained.

Example: Repeated loss of erection during sexual intercourse can set up an expectation of failure at each attempt and when that becomes reality, the erectile dysfunction is thereby maintained.

A raised voice whilst a parent is trying to help with homework when we were young may have caused anger in us. Our partner's ability to explain something to us that we do not understand may evoke the same anger in adult life.

CBT does not seek to predict a course of action before it occurs. It is a tool for making sense of what has already happened. When the behaviour is properly understood, it will involve identifying the predisposing, precipitating or maintaining factors that gave rise to the consequences of the behaviour. During this learning, we can change our cognitions and thus affect the behaviour for the future.

Pavlov experimented with dogs by putting out food and then ringing a bell. What he found was that the hungry dog had observable salivary response to the anticipated food when the dog heard a bell ring summonsing it for food. It anticipated being fed. The ringing of the bell was a conditioned stimulus. The stimulus is paired with the ringing of the bell and being given food, which caused the salivary glands to secrete saliva in anticipation.

During the experiment, Pavlov then changed the method. He started to ring the bell frequently and the dog arrived with the salivary response expecting food, but there was no food. After a while, the salivary response died away, because the dog no longer expected to find food waiting. The pairing was broken. In other words, the ringing of the bell equals food. In anticipation of the food, there was a salivary gland response. When the pairing was broken, the response also changed.

We have all learned inappropriate pairings and associations that have predisposed us, precipitated and caused us to maintain certain types of behaviours. If we can learn more about those predisposing, precipitating and maintaining factors, we are someway towards changing our cognition. As we change our cognition (the way we think, feel and believe), then we start to change our behaviour. So, as we change our mind (our cognition) we can change our life (because we start to change our behaviours as well). What we think is who we are.

Where the mind is, the heart will follow. Changing what the mind thinks will also change what the heart follows.

Recognise that if a stimuli has been present for a long time and a behaviour follows, constant repetition means reinforcement has been taking place over the years and habit has set in. Habit is not just something we do. It is based on stimuli that creates automatic thoughts, beliefs, feelings and then behaviours.

If the stimuli is removed from a particular situation, it can also increase the likelihood of a behaviour occurring. In other words behaviours can have positive reinforcement or negative reinforcement. They are both the same, in that they still reinforce the behaviour.

An example of a negative reinforcement is the absence of praise that used to be present. In response, the person may start to increase their cigarette smoking, which previously they had reduced and got praise for their reduction. The withdrawal of the praise/the stimuli has actually negatively reinforced the continuation of the behaviour.

If a stimulus is removed from a situation, which causes the behaviour to stop, then the behaviour has been extinguished. Recognise, however, that removing a stimulus can cause an increase in the unwanted behaviour.

For example: a mother stops praising the older child for playing with his younger sister (stimulus removed) and so he stops playing with her. That is extinction, but not the extinction outcome sought.

Sometimes when the stimulus (which had been reinforcing the behaviour) is removed, initially the behaviour will increase (because of negative reinforcement), but actually when the stimulus remains absent for a period of time, it eventually results in extinction of the behaviour. In other words, it takes time for the right outcome to be achieved, as there is adaptation to the removal of the stimulus.

If, for example, the older child's mother gave him attention by playing with him when he was being good, as well as ignoring him when he pushed his sister over, the less desirable behaviour would probably have been extinguished quicker.

In CBT, wherever possible the focus is actually to ignore the old behaviour. By ignoring it, you are removing all stimuli that kept the behaviour going, with the intention of extinguishing that old behaviour. At the same time/simultaneously – a new focus of thought, feeling, belief and behaviour in another direction, will positively reinforce a new behaviour. The old and the new will have difficulties continuing side by side. One must get less as the other gets more.

An important principle of learning is that in order to achieve behavioural change, the desired behaviour needs to be broken down into small manageable steps. It is achievement of success at each small manageable step that acts as a positive reinforcement to go on and continue to the next step. Therefore, the new thoughts and behaviours have to be designed in a way that they are undertaken in small manageable steps.

Frequently, failure is because the step undertaken to change a behaviour was too large. The learning that comes out of the process has beneficial effects in other aspects of life. The skills can be used repeatedly.

Chapter 10

Preparing for oneness: Pre-marriage preparation

If it is that meaningful and fulfilling marriages are achieved over a period of time, what are some of the things that we need to learn now in order to be equipped? What problems are brought to the relationship by being unprepared and perhaps immature, self centred, hypercritical, me me!, impatient, competitive, striving for status, seeking self worth and value, insecurity, instability, false or high expectations?

People change as they mature and get older. We all go through life stages and changes. What problems might this bring? Changed perspective, changed levels of friendship and intimacy and changed expectations are just some and they may be welcomed or not so welcomed.

This is what pre-marriage counselling might entail. Below is a form of questionnaire that at the first session, the couple are given and asked to complete it at home without each discussing their replies with the other. They are to bring the completed questionnaire with their written answers to each of the six or so sessions. This is the questionnaire below:

Example of a Pre-marriage expectations Survey

1. LOVE EXPECTATIONS

a) What is your idea of being loved by your partner?

b) Mention two instances of how your partner demonstrated love, during the past one month

c) Mention two instances or situations when your partner made you feel unloved in the past one month

d) Mention two instances or situations when you feel you made your partner feel unloved in the past one month

e) Mention two instances or situations when you think you may have upset your partner in the past 3 months

f) Mention two features of your partner that you sometimes find unattractive

g) Mention two ways in which you think you can help your partner to grow and develop in love for you

h) Have you and your partner discussed the meaning of your marriage commitment?

2. STRENGTHS AND WEAKNESSES

a) Mention two of your strengths and two of your weaknesses

b) Mention two of your partner's strengths and two of their weaknesses

c) Mention at least two ways how you can assist your partner overcome their weaknesses

d) Mention two ways in which you think you can help to develop your partner's strengths

e) Mention two qualities in your partner that you find attractive

f) Mention two features of your partner that you sometimes find unattractive

3. IN-LAWS AND EXTENDED FAMILY

a) Mention two things about your partner's parents you like

b) List three things about your partner's parent you see as potential issues

c) Do you feel fully accepted by your partner's family or are there things that make you uncomfortable?

d) Do you have concerns that either of your families will interfere too much in your upbringing of children?

e) Are there likely to be problems because of the difference in the social, economic, values, beliefs or lifestyle of your two families?

f) Have you discussed and agreed which traditions and customs each will bring from your families into the marriage?

4. MONEY AND FINANCES

a) Have you discussed and decided how you will divide responsibilities for managing your finances and what are they?

b) Have you discussed whether you will have separate or joint bank accounts?

c) Have you discussed how and who will handle your budget?

d) Have you discussed future financial security, such as insurance, savings and investments and wills?

e) Have you discussed the use you will make of credit in your financial management?

f) Do you have concerns that your expenses will exceed your income?

g) Have you discussed whether both of you will work, full time, part-time or give up work?

h) Have you discussed and agreed a maximum figure that either of you may spend without prior discussion with the other?

5. SEX AND SEXUAL ADJUSTMENT

a) Define SEX

b) Do you think that your family had a positive attitude toward sex?

c) Do you have any concerns about a past sexual experience and how it could affect your marriage?

d) What does intimacy mean to you?

e) Are you both able to talk openly about your sexual fears, hopes, desires and preferences?

f) Have you discussed family planning issues and what are your views about family planning?

g) What questions would you ask a knowledgeable person about sex?

6. CHILDREN AND PARENTING

a) Have you discussed whether or not you will have children?

b) Have you discussed whether or not you will be willing to foster or adopt children and what is your view?

c) What would be your ideal number of children?

d) Have you discussed and agreed on the values and beliefs that you will teach your children?

e) Have you discussed how you were disciplined as a child?

f) Have you discussed how each of you will discipline your own children?

g) Have you agreed how soon you will have children (if any)?

h) Have you discussed who will stay home from work if you have children and for how long?

i) If either of you have any children from an earlier marriage/relationship, have you discussed the practicalities around the integration of that child?

7. COMMUNICATION

a) What does "communication" in marriage mean to you?

b) Do you find it difficult to say sorry?

c) Mention two things that up to now you have found difficult to share with your partner.

d) How do you think you might deal with an impasse ó where you cannot agree on something?

e) Would your partner say that you are a good listener?

f) Are there times when you feel unable to share with your partner?

g) Do you have a tendency "to keep the peace" at any price?

h) Do you recognise any past hurts/issues that may cause difficulties in the relationship?

i) Do you feel that you can depend upon your partner for emotional support at all times?

j) Do you know what times of the day is the best or worst time for you both to communicate about important issues?

k) Discuss the ways that your family solved problems.

8. SPIRITUALITY AND VALUES

a) Are there areas of disagreement between you about spiritual or moral issues?

b) Have you discussed and agreed on the extent of your on-going involvement in spiritual/church activities?

c) Do you agree on the amount of financial support each should contribute to the church and charity?

d) Have you discussed and agreed on the activities and practices that will support and strengthen your spiritual growth?

e) Do you have a separate or joint devotional bible reading and prayer time?

f) Mention two of your core values that you live by.

g) Mention two of your partner's core values that they live by.

h) Where you cannot reach agreement over a particular matter, mention the likely options that you will take.

i) What will you do if you later on discover that your marriage relationship is not proceeding along biblical lines?

j) How important is church attendance to you?

9. ROLE EXPECTATIONS

a) How do you see your role in the marriage?

b) How do you see your partner's role in the marriage?

c) Are you in full agreement with your partner's occupation and career plans?

d) Do you have separate or mutual close friends?

e) Will you retain those separate or have only mutual friends?

f) Are there ways in which your partner could show more affection to you?

g) Do you have any concerns about your partner's intake of alcohol, tobacco or drugs?

h) Do you have any concerns about your partner's excess in undertaking sports, hobbies, watching TV, reading or other pastimes?

i) Are there things about your pastime which you will change after you are married?

j) Was there any domestic violence in your previous relationships or family?

k) Has there been any domestic violence with your partner?

l) What is your view about having a protected evening every week for the two of you?

m) Do you feel safe and secure in the relationship?

n) Do you have any concerns about your partner's expression of anger?

Here is what the six or so sessions might include:

Session one:

> Let's talk about you: Getting to know the couple (background, faiths, interests, hobbies, friend housing needs, holidays, children, work, career, ambitions).
>
> - Why get married?
> - Why pre-marriage counselling? Mutual aims and objects.

(After session one, the couple are given the questionnaire below for completion. It is a pre-marriage expectations Survey).

Session two:

> - A Biblical view of marriage.
> - The Genesis 2: 18-24 design - for one man and one woman.
> - The Permanence of marriage (Matthew 19: 3-9).

- That submission thing - in marriage (Ephesians 5: 22-33).

(Commence discussions of the Pre-marriage Expectations Survey)

Sessions three and four:

Continue discussing the Pre-marriage expectations Survey.

Session five:

- The meaning of love (1 Corinthians 13: 1 - 8); the Five Loves.
- Basic sexual anatomy
- Spiritual and moral interpretation of sexual relationship' responsibilities of husband/wife

Session six:

- The wedding ceremony and plans.
- Legal requirements.
- Costs and expenses.
- The Honeymoon.
- Other practical matters.

(Consider giving the option to meet again two months after the wedding and set a definite date)!

Chapter 11

Sex therapy: How can a sex therapist help?

What or who are sex therapists, a sexologist or a psychosexual therapist? They are trained therapists who help people with their sexual problems, using therapeutic methods. It is relatively young amongst the psychological therapies. Sex therapy is available to singles and couples.

It is a difficult and challenging thing indeed, to actually take the step to contact a sex therapist, and the sex therapist will understand that and seek to put you at ease.

It is a privilege to be invited as a guest into peoples lives and go on a journey with them with the aim of achieving better outcomes for them in their lives; or at least to enhance their ability to maximise their potential to achieve better outcomes.

Here are some useful working guidelines which are prerequisites for a couple to be accepted to undergo a programme of sex therapy with a sex therapist:

- The sexual problem (which we shall also call the issue or dysfunction) has remained problematic for at least six months or so;
- There are no ongoing major psychiatric, addictive or abuse patterns – such as domestic violence, alcohol or drug abuse; no

affairs/third party involvement which is still ongoing.
- The woman is not pregnant. Hormonal body changes can adversely affect the dynamics. Post delivery would be the better time to commence sex therapy treatment.
- The sexual issue is the predominant problem, even if there are other secondary issues (which the therapist will assess).
- The general relationship is sufficiently harmonious to be able to sustain the sex therapy homework/loving sessions – which require mutual co-operation and compliance – which becomes more testing as the work unfolds.
- Both have a minimum level of motivation to at least begin the work and a desire to resolve the sexual issue. Motivation is critical. The therapist cannot take ownership of the drive and desire for change. (Some work can be done with just one party who is interested in effecting some improvement).
- Both are willing to set aside time for the work at home and that will require a minimum of three one hour sessions per week and perhaps for six months or more.
- The tasks that the couple will undertake at home, require a cooperative approach for them to resolve the sexual problem. Both should want to work at improving the sexual problem

- Therapy sessions will likely be one hour weekly sessions and perhaps reduce to less frequency at an appropriate point in their progress.
- There should be no use of substances, whether alcohol, drugs or other, before sessions or during the homework to be carried out at home. Neither should substance abuse be a feature of the relationship and so there should be no ongoing treatment for any such problem. All of these interfere with sexual sensitivity and enjoyment.

What does sex therapy entail and look like in practice?

Sex therapists provide a service to individuals and couples in situations where the sexual problem is the main and not the secondary problem in the relationship. Where there are other primary issues causing dissatisfaction in the relationship, then couple counselling may be warranted, rather than sex therapy. Sex may have become entangled in the couples other problems, but not be the primary cause of conflict. To improve the likelihood of sex therapy being beneficial, the couple's general relationship must be "good enough". In other words, is stable, even if conflictual at times.

The presence of a third person (or inanimate other) in the relationship will be contra-indicated for sex therapy. "Inanimate other" refers to ongoing compulsions and addictions through other sexual outlets such as cybersex, Internet pornography, mobile phone sexual activities and the likes – where the process becomes a personified third person with their tentacles in the relationship. That can well be viewed as an affair, even if devoid of an actual person and instead take the form of using inanimate objects for sexual outlet.

The therapist can carry parties secrets which the other does not know about, but that will be the subject of discussion with each privately and for the therapist to judge with each party whether secrets held might get in the way of the therapeutic process. The assessment may involve referral to medical personnel (in certain circumstances) to undertake a particular medical examination in order to rule out physical causes that contribute to the sexual problem.

There will never be any intimate visualisation of body parts during any therapy sessions – as therapists are not necessarily medically qualified and are not practising medicine. Sessions are likely to be weekly unless there are particular restrictions and limitations.

Sexuality is a part of human physiology; is a very personal and sensitive matter for most people and how it is expressed. The expression of sexuality does not always come naturally in a loving marriage bond and at times it needs help more than is recognised - for many couples and individuals.

In our sex saturated society, the expectation is that we all know where to go and what needs to be done to sort out any sexual problem. That is not the entire truth. Many do not know where to go to find and receive help or what the help will look like.

These are some of the sexual problems (seen as dysfunctions) that are treated in sex therapy:

- Lack of desire
- Male erectile dysfunction
- Premature ejaculation
- Lack of orgasm or inhibited orgasm by the man or woman
- Dyspareunia – pain for either party upon attempt to insert the penis into the vagina
- Vaginismus – involuntary female muscle contractions makes it difficult or impossible to insert the penis into the vagina
- Sexual arousal issues
- Sexual aversion – perhaps anxiety or disgust at aspects of the sexual act
- Vulvodynia (previously termed Vestibulitis) – Vulvar discomfort or pain where there is no major anatomic or neurologic findings for the discomfort.

Sex therapy may be very useful for those with particular physical disabilities and also for the elderly – where sex should and can continue to be enjoyed. Post surgery and other surgically necessitated impairments can benefit well from sex therapy.

There will be a very extensive general and sexual history taking process from both parties on separate occasions, before coming to a working hypothesis/diagnosis and then the preparation of a flexible and adaptable treatment plan or program which the couple will follow for a period which may well exceed six months of weekly sessions.

A very extensive general and sexual history is a prerequisite for the sex therapist's ability to diagnose and offer a working hypothesis or diagnosis of what has caused or contributed to and is maintaining the sexual issue or dysfunction.

Sensate focus

Do please remember that there is no substitute for undertaking sensate focus exercises as a part of a structured sex therapy program with a skilled practitioner. It is hard to replicate the exercises too quickly after self help attempts at doing them. The brain can quickly sabotage second attempts.

There follows a rudimentary outline only. Remember that this tool comes with a health warning! It is not recommended as a self-help DIY tool. The brain will remember the exercises which prejudice being able to use the sensate program again for quite a period after last completing a program. It is a program of personally tailored exercises (better called loving sessions) that the couple undertakes at home. One-hour sessions, three times per week is the minimum time period required.

When sexual intercourse is just not working, it is better to cease. Why? Because the brain is programmed to react to repeated behaviours. That creates habits. It remembers good and bad experiences and they are stored. Bad experiences set it up to expect another repeated bad outcome even before you try. It is ready in anticipation. It is working against you and not for you. We need to reprogram it with some repeatedly good outcomes so that it anticipates and expects good outcomes.

Sensate focus is an exercise regime in a cognitive behavioural therapy program. The couple agree to a ban on any further attempts at sexual intercourse until directed by the therapist. That is mandatory. The couple then need to start again to relearn every aspect of the others body through touch. They take turn being first active in giving to the other and then passive, where they receive from the other person. The purpose is to enable the couple to gain and also increase their sensual, as well as sexual, awareness of own and their partner's body responses. All five senses are incorporated – smell, sight, touch, sound and taste. Self-preparation, by washing and room preparation are vital ingredients of the exercise and the couple will be taught how to go about those features of the exercise.

Sensate focus exercises are likely to be incorporated by the couple into their foreplay repertoire at a later stage when they reintroduce sexual intercourse into their pattern of sexual expression. They learn to take responsibility for both giving and also receiving sensations. It begins to eliminate performance anxiety and what we call "spectatoring" in a non-participatory way whilst things are done to them and they are absent in mind or disconnected from the sensations.

There are in fact three stages as follows:

Senate focus I involves the parties learning how to set the scene in the form of self and room preparation, so that all five senses are allowed to take in the occasion. There follows non-genital sensual touching (not intended to be sexual) of each other's bodies in a very well directed manner. All erogenous areas of the body are out of bounds during the soft and light finger touching exercise of each other's body. That includes particularly the genitals. The intention and purpose is not to work at arousing and turning on the other person, but rather for the receiving partner to learn to relax and receive the sensations.

Sensate focus II is introduced at the right time following feedback from the couple and therapist recognizing they are ready to move on to this stage. This stage is also called "Non-demand". The genitals and erogenous zones are included for touch, but only so that the body experiences whole and all over full body sensations. The intention is not, however, aimed at arousal and planned sexual awakening. It still is for taking in and becoming more aware of full body sensations from touch and stroking in a non-demanding way.

The third stage is also called Sensate focus II, but is intentional sexual arousal and still taking sensual and sexual whole body pleasure, but may at this point include massage, introduced at any earlier stage. Specific other treatment strategies will then be introduced, having been individually designed in the treatment plan for that couple, dependent upon the sexual issue being addressed.

Self focus exercises

It is common to introduce additional and individual work for one or both, in the form of self-focus exercises. The purpose of such exercises is to help either of the individuals to learn to become comfortable with their own body, to become aware of the sensations of their own body and thereafter, increase their ability to give feedback to their partner at the appropriate stage when permitted by the therapist in the sensate focus work.

Relaxation exercise

The couple will be taught how to incorporate forms of relaxation exercises before doing any of the other exercises, as and when each may need it, in order to relax them in preparation to put down the stresses of their day and prepare to get into the session.

Kegel's exercise for men and for women

At a stage in the sensate focus program, sexual intercourse will be re-introduced. It is well recognized that training and toning up the pelvic muscles for men and women does increase their orgasmic experience when it happens. Regular practice of the Kegel's exercise strengthens the muscles that surround the penis and vagina and does improve circulation of blood in the pelvis, all of which have been reported as producing stronger and more pleasurable orgasms.

The exercise is non-intrusive since it can be done anywhere at any time. It involves identifying and isolating the pelvis muscles. That can be done by identifying the muscles used to stop urinating mid-flow. Those are the pelvis muscles. The task is to squeeze and release the muscles in a defined way. The number of repetition of squeeze and release is built up and increased daily. Many people can experience the benefits within days.

Chapter 12

What happens during each of the sexual responses cycle phases for both females and males?

In the later chapters, under the five loves, we shall again look at the sexual response cycle. Here, we look at the anatomical changes which the female and the male body undergoes during each of those stages of Excitement, Plateau, Orgasm and Resolution, as identified by Masters & Johnson and the Desire stage later added by Kaplan. Desire represents a person's general level of interest in sex. The Desire stage is sometimes referred to as sexual interest or libido and is referred to as the first of the stages in women's sexual response cycle. Not so for men, as Desire can frequently be absent – as strange as that may sound.

Let's first look at females:

Desire: Arguably this phase belongs only to females, since males do not need this desire phase and they can start with Excitement - from a standing start so to speak!

Excitement: Heart rate, pulse and blood pressure increase. After only 10 – 20 seconds of sexual stimulation the vagina may produce lubrication, lengthens internally and distend as it gets ready to accommodate the penis. The clitoris becomes erect and the inner and outer lips of the vagina engorge with blood and so increase in size, whilst the uterus begins to elevate. A form of sex flush may appear over the chest and breasts and be quite visible as the breasts swell in size.

Plateau: The tissue around the nipples fill with fluid and the erect nipples may lose their erection. The uterus is fully ascended and the inner and outer vaginal lips open, as the outer third of the vagina engorges with blood and become distended so as to form what is described as the orgasmic platform. The perhaps now sensitive clitoris retracts under its hood.

Orgasm: Most of the body muscles become tense, as heart rate, pulse, blood pressure and breathing increase further. The uterus begins contractions, as well as the pelvic floor muscles at 0.8 second intervals so that the orgasmic platform pulsates from 3 to maybe 15 times.

Resolution: The respiratory system returns to normal rate; the sex flush disappears and muscular contractions cease. The nipples lose their erection and engorgement and the clitoris swelling goes down. The orgasmic platform which was congested with blood, returns to normal rest, as well as swelling in the inner and outer vaginal lips. The uterus descends, but the cervix remains open for a further 20 – 30 minutes after orgasm as its motion causes dipping into the seminal fluid pool. Unlike the male, females can repeat the phases straightaway and have repeated orgasms – without a refractory period. All males experience the refractory phase.

Let's now consider the sexual response phases for males:

Excitement: The penis engorges with blood and produces an erection. The nipples may also become erect; breathing rate, heart rate and blood pressure all increase. The skin around the scrotum thickens and the testes rise.

Plateau: Muscular tension increase and a sex flush may also be visible on certain parts of the skin. The urethra increase in diameter and the Cowper's gland produces a clear secretion to lubricate the urethra and cleanse any acidic residue of urine. Some men experience a pre-cum discharge of clear fluid. The Coronal ridge of the penis increases, the testes swell by some 50%, elevate and the penis glans deepen in colour.

Orgasm: Breathing and heart rates, as well as blood pressure increase yet further. There is a feeling of inevitability (where a point is reached when ejaculation cannot be stopped). The Testes contract and sperm travel along the vas deferens in a peristalsis motion, as the seminal vesicles and prostate contract. The anus may also contract. Sperm joins the Seminal fluid to form semen, which is the ejaculate secreted out of the penis at 0.8 second intervals.

Resolution: Not to be ignored, this phase is significant and is the feel good phase when bonding is at its deepest. Something Spiritual occurs and cements that "oneness" which the Bible speaks about. The erection begins to subside. The scrotum relaxes and testes swelling diminishes and descends. Breathing and heart rate, as well as blood pressure return to normal, as muscles relax and any sex flush dissipates.

Note that this period is followed by a **Refractory period** and is unique to males only. For a period of time it is not physically possible for the male to ejaculate again. That Refractory period can vary from just minutes to days and depends upon lots of factors including age, consumption of alcohol, drug intake and other matters.

Fig 1 below is a useful exercise which can be undertaken with the couple in order to tease out discrepancies in their voiced decision about wanting to remain together and work at the relationship. Ulterior or unmatched desires and expectation about the future of the relationship can be teased out by the therapist. Both parties have their own sheet with the pictures and are asked three questions as follows:

- Write "P" in one box only as to which picture best represents to you a time in the PAST when the relationship was at its best for you.
- Write "N" in one box only as to which picture best represents to you a time NOW where the relationship is now for you.
- Write "F" in one box only as to which picture best represents to you what the relationship will look like and be at its best when therapy has been successful –

even if you do not see how it can get to such a place at the moment.

The parties and the therapist can then discuss their respective choices and help the parties to see where the other is at. It will speak volumes and communicate some things which may even contradict what each are voicing verbally.

Fig 1

Collusive fits do change. By that we refer to the conscious and unconscious processes which cause us to gravitate to a partner who then becomes a husband or wife. We all change. Life stages change (because we all get older and mature) causing us to sometimes want different things from the relationship. Problems occur where the two are not in regular and close communication and so respective needs are not well voiced. Old ways can start to wear thin and dissatisfaction sets in, but not voiced to the other, let alone to self.

The goal posts have moved. Sometimes for one partner and at other times, for both. Negotiating new desires, needs and expectations can be very difficult indeed, particularly where communication has waned in recent years and the two have gotten used to living in their own worlds and only meet over common issues such as issues with children, finance and in-laws.

Security in the relationship may be such that one no longer needs to feel touch and tight embrace quite so often – as some of the images depict in fig 1. To communicate such a need to the other may be interpreted as rejection and a falling out of love. It may in fact be a coming of age where tactile inseparable embraces are no longer a prerequisite to enable one (who was previously needed) to explore their independence. That will represent a shift and change. Change can be threatening. Insecurity in the relationship can cause change to enhance any pre-existing chinks.

Chapter 13

What is "Sex Addiction"?

Sex Addiction is also called hypersexuality, ego-dystonic, sexual impulse control disorder, sexual compulsivity or paraphilia and non-paraphilia sexual behaviour. Some compulsive and addictive behaviours include: magazine pornography, internet pornography, cybersex (spending time online focused on sexual or romantic intrigue or involvement), compulsive masturbation, compulsive acting out, male and female escorts and/or prostitutes, chat rooms and social sites, texting sex sites, swinging and/or group sex, multiple flirtation and/or affairs and sex binges.

In a study of extreme cybersex users, those that go on the internet for sexual stimulation, 40% were women[45]. 70% of internet pornography traffic occurs between 9am and 5pm[46]; in other words, during work time. 79% of companies reporting internet misuse by staff, say that it is due to pornography[47].

Hyper sexuality, over sexuality, compulsive sexual behaviour, sexual dependency, sexual addiction, and many more are different terms given to behaviours that arise out of addition to sexually explicit material (SEM).

A study in 1999 of 10000 men and women (of which 83% were men and 17% women), provided some revealing statistics:

- 15%-20% of internet users engage in some form of sexual activity.[48]
- 8% showed signs of sexual compulsivity.[49]
- Men access erotica/porn and women access chat rooms.[50]
- 32% acknowledged that their activity jeopardised at least one important area of their life[51] (in other words, people would take risks to get the pleasure).
- 20% of men and 12% of women admitted using their work computer for some form of sexual activity.[52]

A definition of cybersex is "a social interaction between at least two persons, who are exchanging real time digital messages in order to become sexually aroused and satisfied".[53]

Since it is "virtual" it can be seen as not real and not really hurting anyone. It can be used as an outlet for the disenfranchised to explore their sexuality; in particular, those who cannot form relationships very easily.

Sex addiction takes many forms. What is for sure is that it starts (so we think) to meet a need, which exists within us. Of course, what any addiction does is cover over the need or insecurity for just a period of time and bring with it many,

many other problems – the price of a temporary fix. As with any addiction, what we need to do is find out what is the unmet need; what is the purpose and function that the addictive behaviour serves.

We do not actually see with our eyes, we see with our brains and so for men, it is the visual pictures which provide the best stimulation. Women are rather different. It is the cognitive part of the brain that hears, which provides the best stimulation and so women are more likely to go into chat rooms, rather than look at the internet pornography.

It is a maladaptive pattern of sexual behaviour leading to clinically significant impairment or distress, as manifested by three or more number of key markers over a 12 month period. Various sex addiction tests/screening checklists are available online.

Here though are the critical prerequisites for a diagnosis of Sex Addiction:

> A pattern of sexual behaviours which preoccupy thoughts **and**
>
> those thoughts are out of control **and**
>
> the person cannot stay stopped for a sustainable period or consistently **and**

the behaviour has harmful consequences

and

the behaviour serves a purpose and function in the individual's life.

It is a fact that the behaviour "serves a purpose and function" which denotes it as sex addiction.

Remember at all times when referring to sex and love addiction, we are referring to behaviours, rather than people. In other words, we have people caught up with sex and love addiction behaviours. In truth, we do not have sex and love addicts; we need to separate the addiction from the person, as the addictive behaviour should not define them as a person. An alcoholic has an addictive behaviour to alcohol. He or she is not in truth – an alcoholic.

We need to separate the person from the behaviour, otherwise the person will be "in recovery" for the rest of their life as a recovering alcoholic or sex or love addict. The healing hands of God can therefore never do a fully restoring work in their life because they must always be "in recovery". That cannot be right. The behaviour is separate from the person and as such can be made a permanent separate entity from the person and no longer live with the person.

"Shame" is the driver which maintains sex addiction. It is vital to understand the interplay between shame and guilt in maintaining sex addiction. Addiction and shame are inseparable. Shame and guilt are emotions causing negative self-evaluation. There is a difference between guilt and shame. Guilt says: "This behaviour is bad". Shame says: "I'm a bad person". Try to tackle sex addiction without tackling shame and you are bound to fail! Shame has to be worked through in order to overcome the compulsion. Shame underpins and supports the behaviour and keeps it going. Shame is to compulsion, what oxygen is to fire. It fans and feeds it.

Narcissism is also something that needs to be mentioned, as another trait that underpins and keeps sex addiction active. The symptoms include the feelings of dissatisfaction with self, inferiority, emptiness, boredom, intense envy and chronic uncertainty. If the self feels unaccepted, painful and flawed, something will have occurred early on which set up such things from very early childhood.

We also know that brain development is a significant contributor. Mood altering sensations are enjoyable. Neurochemical changes - which the brain likes - help to cope with the stresses and issues in life. The brain will develop use dependency. Repeated acting out becomes a must. Corrective action is needed at various and different levels to give back conscious and unconscious control of behaviour choices.

Sex and compulsivity for sex is at an epidemic level. Sex compulsivity, sex and use of the Internet, mobile phones and computers are just some of the modern age technologies that have become our "little gods". For some, reliance on them is critical to the well being of their lives. Compulsive behaviours and addiction takes many forms.

What is certain is that it starts because we think we have to meet a need which exists within us. Of course, what any compulsive behaviour does is to plaster over a need or insecurity for just a temporary period of time and afterwards shame and guilt bring with it many, many other problems.

With any compulsion/addiction, what we need to do is find out what the unmet need is. It serves a purpose and a function that not even our love of God seems to be able to fill. Counselling can play an important role.

Addicts risk paying a high price for the pleasures that come from acting out. The real pleasure is not so much the orgasm, but the chase for the ultimate experience. Sex addiction therapy intervention helps us to learn that we can survive without the constant sexual acting out. But don't forget the partners who are affected and need help with the issues as well.

There is a service devoted entirely to helping partners and groups.

What is "Love Addiction"?

Love addiction focuses on love as the solution to inner pain, loneliness and emptiness by creating relationships or romance which are consuming pastimes. It could be defined as an attempt to regulate one's mood by getting and having the positive regard of someone else.

Someone once said, *"The chief cause of unhappiness is trading what we want most for what we want at the moment"*. In William Shakespeare's "Twelfth Night", Duke Orsino is upset that his courtship attempt with Olivia is not going well and asks for an abundance of love so that he will lose his appetite. He was in love with the idea of being in love. He says:

"If music be the food of love, play on;
Give me excess of it, that, surfeiting,
The appetite may sicken, and so die."[54]

Love addiction is coined as a phase referring more to women's activities (as distinct from viewing pornography). A modern day symptom is well illustrated by the addictive use of the social media to meet others and develop relationships with potential partners, no matter how fleeting the contact.

The love addicts have very intense emotions including anger, fear, hate and love for the other person. At its root, it hides issues of insecure bonding and attachment to a significant carer, often a mother, throughout childhood. In all respects it is an addiction that requires treatment in therapy.

Sex and love addicts usually have multiple other addictions. Work on one addiction inadequately and other addictions surface or re-surface, such as gambling addiction, alcoholism and alcohol addiction, alcohol abuse, drug abuse, drug addiction, substance abuse, heroin addiction, cocaine addiction and food addiction.

Alongside one to one therapy sessions, the addicts are encouraged to attend a 12 steps program. Programs such as Sex and Love Addicts Anonymous are worldwide and operate like Alcoholics Anonymous. The intention is to achieve and maintain sobriety – which means a total abstinence from acting out. The group dynamics, and the support such a group offers, is just one of the benefits of a 12 steps program.

The Brain and neural pathways

A neural pathway is a network of neurons in the brain which are responsible for the automation of emotions, feelings and behaviours. Learning is a result of neural pathway formation in the brain. The greater the repetition and the greater the duration, the greater the learning.

Negative neural pathway formations include anger, learned anxiety and phobias. Other examples of neural pathway formation include learning to play an instrument, learning a new language and motor development. When the environment is set up, the same reactive behaviour will be reproduced and manifest itself. They operate at an unconscious level.

The brain develops in a use dependency way. In other words, use it or lose it. Lack of use will diminish your ability to do something. Even unhealthy coping strategies are neural pathways that have carved out a place. The compulsion or habit is working from an existing template and so does not need a conscious decision on your part to activate the behaviour. Relearning is possible in order to create healthier neural pathways. It is called Cognitive Neural Restructuring Therapy (CNRT). Sounds very grand, but it is essentially a form of CBT work.

We all learned coping mechanisms to handle stress, tiredness, boredom, loneliness, anxiety and other such feelings. Most of those strategies are maladaptive and aimed at self-soothing. We need to learn new strategies that are more effective.

Sexual Map & Sexual Template

We develop a sexual template from quite a young age and practice of that template results in individuals evolving a sexual map of likes, desires and preferences (whether they are in the range of acceptability or not). A love map (also known as a sexual map) is an individual's unique erotic signature.

The brain plays a key part in that evolving sexuality, sexual map and sexual template. Understanding the rudimentary functioning of aspects of the brain is useful in knowing why the brain is not a person's best friend when there is an attempt to change habits, compulsive practices and addictions.

This smart part of the brain is known as the cerebral cortex. It directs us what to do in a given situation through reasoning. It does know how to avoid compulsion and addictions. Then there is the limbic system, which is the emotional part of the brain, comprising the amygdala, hippocampus, thalamus and nucleus accumbens.

The amygdala affects bodily needs such as anger, eating, sex and responses such as fight and flight. It develops before the hippocampus. It responds to visual stimuli. The hippocampus sorts out what is relevant to store in the memory. It is not fully developed at birth, until a much later age. The thalamus directs the sensory signals from the spinal cord to the cerebral cortex. The nucleus accumbens is the pleasure centre and also ensures life sustaining activities are maintained. Dopamine is released in this pleasure zone.

The Cycle of an addiction

This is what the cycle of any addiction looks like and applies equality to issues such as masturbation and other compulsive behaviours:

The Cycle of Addiction

Fig 2

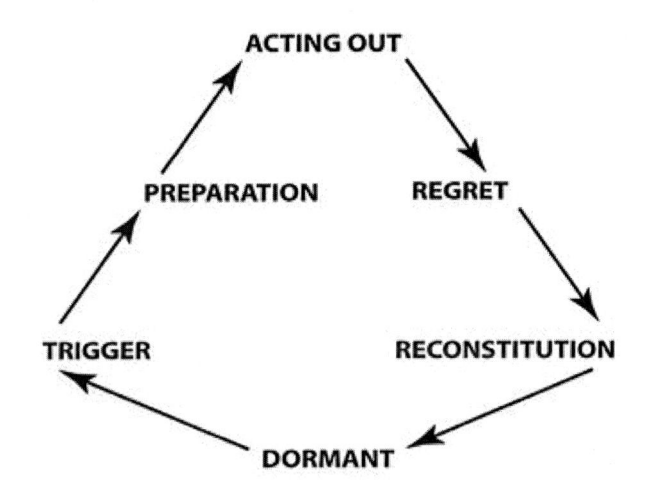

```
              ACTING OUT
             ↗          ↘
    PREPARATION        REGRET
        ↑                  ↘
    TRIGGER           RECONSTITUTION
          ↖            ↙
              DORMANT
```

ACTING OUT: *The act of masturbation, with or without aids such as fantasising and/or porn and/or objectifying women visually.*

REGRET: *Guilt, shame and feeling sinful before God.*

RECONSTITUTION: *Make massive effort not to do it again by resolving and will power.*

DORMANT: *Loneliness, boredom, anger, frustration*

TRIGGER: objectifying women or men with eyes, *opportunity presents, feeling lonely, bored, lonely and without a close other person to share life; feeling unvalued.*

PREPARATION: *rationalisation, blame, fault of others, everyone does it; I am entitled, minimizing the effects and consequences*

The partners are affected as well

…and do not forget the partners of sex and love addiction. Here is a copy of my information sheet which I provide to enquirers of what work with them can look like:

He "caused" our problems and yet once again the focus and everyones attention is on him. The family income is being used by him again for his benefit, on top of the spend he has already enjoyed on his addiction. It's just not fair. I am left here with his stuff and don't know where to go or turn for help for me. That just is not right and is not fair. I feel so.....

This is an understandable reframe, don't you think? It is right? Well - mostly - yes! But there is help for female partners of sex addicts.

Partner or wife of a judge, a solicitor, a barrister, an accountant, a teacher, an IT consultant, a utilities operator, a facilities manager, a HR personnel, a company director, an actor. Whichever of these male personnel to whom you are in a relationship with, sex addiction can have its tentacles into your relationship with them. It can leave you carrying a very heavy burden, with few people there for you to talk to about this world which has taken a toll on your relationship and continues to undermine it.

Will it ever get better? Can he really stop the behaviours? Will I ever be able to trust him again? How do I know the children are safe? How do I compete with that stuff? Was it my fault or did I contribute? Was I not enough or not good enough? How could I have been so stupid? How is it that I did not heed the signs that I now look back on and can see them? What do I do now? Do I really believe there is such a thing as sex addiction? Isn't it just greed for more sex? Where can I turn for help? What if people find out? How can I bear to carry this on my own?

I am scared to join some form of women's group. Their problems are not like mine. What if it gets out? My husband won't agree to me attending a group. He is getting his help, but I have to hold on in there and not tell anyone in case.

It's just not right. It's just not fair. This is my life. He has ruined it. What am I going to do?

There is as yet only a handful of women's support group for partners of sex addicts. What does such a group do and look like? It is highly confidential, with numbers of between 5 to 8 women. They may perhaps be 12 weeks in length and 1½ hour sessions.

What does the program look like? Teaching and discussion can centre on the following:

- Definition of sex addiction and love addiction
- Common understandable error patterns which partners fall into and battles you will lose
- The role of the addiction
- Partner's absolute "No No's"
- What can we learn about "Adult/Parent/Child" ego state interactions
- Family of origin, family scripts, contributors and what set up the addiction
- Effect on the stars - Hollywood, Professionals, the good and the great, across the board - all are susceptible
- Evolution of the sexual template and map
- Cycle of addiction
- Boundaries
- Trust, money, healthy sexuality
- Self responsibility and self care
- Own support groups
- Attachment, Shame, Narcissism, Co-dependency
- Grief cycle
- Questions women ask
- Hope, fears and reservations
- Disclosure or not - and extent of disclosure to family and the children
- Legality issues
- Restoring the relationship or leaving the relationship

- Recommended reading

Shame, resistance and blocks will work against many female partners attending a group. Yet group therapy may well be the best type of therapy for ongoing support, so crucial in sex addiction recovery for partners.

Chapter 14

Errors of pastoral workers and Christian Counsellors who counsel those with sex addiction behaviours

The treatment of sex and love addiction is a specialized area of therapy, and a high level of knowledge and competency is expected of those seeking to help clients negotiate this terrain; otherwise further damage can be done. The Lord may work His healing miracle in such a process. That will always obviate the need for counselling. What the Lord does, he does very well indeed.

We carry an awesome responsibility as therapists, as we are invited into the most intimate of places in a client's life. Consider what John Wood has to say:

"I will present you parts of myself slowly

if you are patient and tender; I will open drawers that mostly stay closed

and bring out places and people and things, sounds

and smells, loves and frustrations,

hopes and sadnesses,

bits and pieces of three decades of life that have been grabbed off in chunks

and found lying in my hands.

> *They have eaten their way into my memory*
>
> *carved their way into my heart altogether*
>
> *... you or I will never see them ...*
>
> *They are me.*
>
> *If you regard them lightly, deny they are important*
>
> *or worse, judge them*
>
> *I will quietly, slowly*
>
> *begin to wrap them up in small pieces of velvet*
>
> *like worn silver and gold jewelry,*
>
> *tuck them away in a small wooden chest of drawers*
>
> *and close."*[55]

The problem is that when the drawer does close, it may remain closed for decades before a client gains the confidence to again try to trust someone in their cry for help.

Christians are most likely to seek help from a "Christian counsellor". There are far too few Christians, who become counsellors, and are willing and comfortable to practice in this field; yet the need is great. Unwittingly, much further damage is done by those who are well-meaning and seek to transfer a skill set from one area of therapy into this area. It is an oversight to treat the addiction as moral failure and not as a mental health issue with a true disease categorisation.

This is an area where church members are perhaps the most unforgiving. Sex addiction is just not understood and so compassion and empathy can be lacking. There is a sense of having brought it upon self and is excess sex gone wrong and out of control, causing betrayal to others. Moral outrage yields no place of refuge for those who dare to seek help and so are forced to suffer silently and the inevitable exposure is what brings them to the fore, by which time major damage has been done to self and others.

Lack of knowledge by the counsellor and the fact of the client being thrust upon them (often at a time of crisis) can evoke a sense of being out of one's depth and so quickly revert to the little they do know about the subject. A genuine determination to help may, however, not be good enough to progress the recovery journey. The counsellor needs to seek guidance.

There can be a misguided juxtapositioning of sex addiction behaviours as including paedophilia and with that can be an inappropriate heavy-handed approach to protect perceived vulnerable children. That can unhelpfully endorse the misguided view of a female partner, who wrongly reacts to protect the children from perceived abuse. The thinking then is about the need to evoke safeguarding procedures. Other agencies may then be consulted – often very unnecessarily. They become involved and confidence is broken on a perceived "need to know basis" by sharing material disclosed by the addict.

Those clergy expected to uphold the highest level of sexual purity (in the ministry) have few places to rest their head when issues come out about their behaviours. Treble jeopardy means loss of position, ministry, career, manse, standing in the church, community, income and a lot lot more. How then does a partner, who knows of the behaviours, confide in anyone? It is simply far too risky and dangerous to the household.

Children looking on and seeing how a parent is then treated by the church using its best endeavor are traumatized and, as a future consequence, many want nothing further to do with such an organisation. Could it be that many of those caught up in the process eventually leave the Church and their hurt cause them to renounce any part Christ and the Church will play in their life. They (whether the ostracized leader, wife or children) may later become lesbian, gay, bisexual & transgender (LGBT) members, who carry a vendetta against the church. They become a vocal spokesperson against all things religious.

The fact is that sex addiction behaviours are very prevalent in Christian circles, Christians' lives, the Ministry and those within Churches' head offices and amongst senior clergy. It is prevalent in the pews and pulpit alike. Why? It is not about sex. It is a behavior trait and practices learned (not always sexual at that point) from childhood and triggered at puberty, adolescence or adulthood, as a coping tragedy. It is used to soothe away and make better (albeit temporarily) the excess of life's intolerable feelings. It is a maladaptive strategy which the brain gravitates toward, but has its roots in childhood.

The very real potential exists in the role of clergy to exhibit sex addiction behaviours. Consider the terrain within which they work. Giving themselves out emotionally, day after day, with perhaps insufficient coming back in; week after week, month after month, year after year; carrying others deepest confidences and no outlet in the form of supervision, where they can take their own stuff and have someone else who is there to look after their emotional well-being.

During a time when they have run dry, they can find themselves taking solace in sex addiction behaviours. The brain, which gets a high from the activity, uses cognitive distortions (untrue reasoning) to justify, normalise, transfer blame, deny, minimise, rationalise and magnify entitlement to do the behaviours.

What are the behaviours? Internet porn viewing, porn magazines, visiting prostitutions, gay sex, cybersex and using webcams are just some of the myriad of "acting out" practices and behaviours. Technology has become the master rather than remain the servant.

There is much to learn from secular therapists in this evolving, relatively new, fertile and developing field of practice. There are times when the Lord does not perform His miracle of healing in the sex addict's life in an instantaneous way - but rather they have to go through a process of healing in a *precept upon precept, line by line, here a little, there a little* - progressive way.

Here are some of the errors and oversights which Christian counsellors and pastoral workers (whether clergy or otherwise) have unwittingly made and which may have caused a regrettable legacy of further damage:

The sex addiction therapist knows well that any therapy MUST include a partner. A partner (whether a husband or more usually a wife) will have suffered trauma when finding out about the behaviours. The partner also needs care and attention in their recovery journey. Sadly, so often little or no attention is given to a partner of a sex addict. Their trauma (of learning about the behaviours) are further heightened as they see the addict spending the family budget on therapy, getting all the attention and help and yet the addict was the cause of the relationship trauma.

Sexual sin is regarded as the worst sin and such individuals are often shunned in a very subtle Christian way. Forgiveness is voiced, but not experienced in reality in many Christian circles. Grace from onlookers can be very far away for the person with sex addiction behaviours, particularly for those in senior or leadership roles where the standards expected are much higher. That keeps the lid on any thoughts of confiding and sharing each other's burdens. The addiction behavior, unwittingly is enabled and empowered to thrive in that environment.

If you are a female Christian, caught up in such behaviours, they might be over pathologised as having other deficits, beyond those that cause the equivalent male christian to fall into such a male orientated activity! Inaccurate and incomplete information can be harmful and have harmful consequences. Not recognising the concept of co-addiction and working with it at the right time can alienate and place greater levels of guilt and unhealthy shame upon the partner. Unhealthy shame and guilt are the very traits that hold the sex addicts behaviours in place and are thereby being transferred onto the partner.

A model of casting the addict into the role of the sick patient who must be healed and the partner as a victim misses any co-dependency behaviours present in the relationship. It means that the sick patient is very sinful and responsible for the ills in the marriage. The victim is therefore virtuous and an innocent sufferer who deserves the support. Where her own therapy and self-recovery is not prioritized, it will leave her with a deep wound that remains open and oozing. Trauma therapy is indicated for her.

Ignoring the possibility of co-dependency is misguided. The addiction may have been unwittingly maintained by the system in which each party lived life and behaved one toward the other. A female partner may try harder to become more sexual so that the addict does not need or want to look outside the relationship. It is her attempt to fight back for her husband. Implicit in her attempt is the reasoning that she must have unwittingly contributed to him developing the behavior. Therefore her availability for more sex and more adventurous "Ann Summers" gadget sex with her will cure him. That it is deeply flawed and sets her up for another betrayal and trauma.

A female partner already has a severely limited number of supports around her, with whom she can confide for help. The counsellor may suggest containment of the issues in order to protect the reputation of a key church leader, role model or personnel and thereby neutralise the limited support that the female partner may have. That increases her sense of total isolation, carrying the burden of the unforgivable of all church indiscretions.

Female Sex addicts are likely to be judged more harshly than males. There must be something more fundamentally flawed in a woman who behaves in this way. She cannot deserve to have children in her household.

To encourage her to monitor his behavior is to further damage her self-esteem, respect and integrity – which are already at an all time low. What these activities will do is to bolster up, enhance and maintain any co-dependency. Setting up a wife to become the husband's accountability partner, so that she knows what he is thinking and acting upon, is unhelpful. It changes the relationship dynamic in an adverse way. The female partner is cast into the parent role and the male addict is the child. The potential for her to be re-traumatised is very real.

Shaming of the male addict is enhanced. The very thing that underpins sex addiction behavior is further fuelled to a higher degree, thereby keeping it active and repeating the cycle of addiction.

Viewing the behaviours through only a religious lens may mean the focus for help is on the sole basis of "sexual sin". That may mean adopting a stance whereby all sexual sin should be dealt with in only one particular way, involving confession, repentance and abstinence. Sex addiction behavior is, by its nature a repetitive, long term habit underpinned by secrecy. The practice does not just stop and go away. Treating the behaviours as open to spiritual resolve only and not acknowledging the role that the cognitive, emotional and neurochemical aspects play in servicing the addiction, can set the addict up for much distress and relapse.

Repentance is, of course, right. It may be, however, that other corrective measures are needed in addition to spiritual ones. CBT to change cognition in order to change behaviour practices is also required.

There will have been a neurochemical impact because of the regular release of those neurochemicals into the pleasure zone of the brain. The effects of neurochemicals released impacting the brain is as potent as illegal drugs in the body and to ignore that fact is to do a disservice to the person with the sex addiction behaviours. The impact of relapse on the sex addict can be debilitating, because relapse was not contemplated. Repeated sin and relapse can be interpreted as insufficient willpower or conviction by the struggler.

A psychodynamic review of the role the family of origin and upbringing played, may be seen as opening up an otherwise closed and no-go area in a person's life because of past forgiveness and closure. It may be seen as dishonouring to father and mother to raise any implicit criticism about the role parents played in the early childhood nurturing stage and therefore an understanding of the crucial "purpose and function" which the addiction plays, can be missed. Unrecognised and untreated, the function and purpose may be fulfilled through the back door by gravitating to a different type of compulsion and addiction activity.

Prescribed medication may be a causative adverse effect, which is easily ignored. Attendance at a 12 steps program may be seen as something to be avoided and may deny the person of what could be a very significant support and necessary group therapy. At its core, a 12 steps program recognises the need for personal responsibility, repentance, transformation and acknowledgement of someone bigger than self.

After the revelation, it is wise to look at the continued sexual expression in the couple relationship. New boundaries may be required for a period (and thereby restrict the availability of sexual expression within the couple relationship). Many may be hesitant to put in place such tighter boundaries and stopping the sexual contact between a man and his wife, for fear of doing something contrary to Biblical teaching. Yet that is what may be necessary – for a season.

The full extent of his acting out may not yet be known. He may have contracted a sexually transmitted infection. Without prior testing, his wife is exposed. Abstinence for a season is a wise precaution.

To not believe a man's promise not to do it again can be turned on the woman as unscriptural unforgiveness and cause her to feel ostracised. Divorcing the sinful husband and moving on, leaves issues unresolved with any co-dependency trait in her, likely to raise its head again in a future relationship. The counsellor unwittingly colludes with the disease to keep it in place in both of them.

An inner healing type course can be effective in breaking iniquity and not just sin and set the captive free in an instance without counselling. The Holy Spirit can and does work in that way, thus making therapy redundant. That is the best treatment!

There are times, however, when the Holy Spirit does not perform an instant miracle in some peoples lives and there is a need for them to go through a process; a process of therapy for their healing. It is nonetheless healing in every way, in the hands of a well-trained competent sex addiction therapist. It will mean longer term therapy and coming to terms with incremental change - "precept upon precept, line upon line, line upon line, here a little, there a little" (Is 28: 10).

When it comes to CBT (Cognitive Behaviour Therapy), the Bible got there first. After all, these verses are CBT practices - invented long long ago:

"And do not be conformed to this world, but be transformed by the renewing of your mind, that you may prove what is that good and acceptable and perfect will of God" – Rom 12: 2

"Finally, brethren, whatever things are true, whatever things are noble, whatever things are just, whatever things are pure, whatever things are lovely, whatever things are of good report, if there is any virtue and if there is anything praiseworthy - meditate on these things." - <u>Philippians 4:7-9</u>.

If you can change your mind, you can change your life. That principle is all about renewing the mind. That which occupies the cognition is what we will go on to practice. Therefore changed thinking equals changed action and practices.

There are those who have been practicing in the treatment of sex addiction for a few decades now and advocated the inclusion of it in the manual which categorises all mental health conditions. That manual is used all over the world and is abbreviated and called DSM V. Available evidence-based practice has not convinced those concerned that sex addiction has come of age so as to yet include it. Those therapists who witness the good outcomes, are clear that it should be included.

PART TWO

Chapter 15

SONG OF SOLOMON AS A PATTERN FOR LOVERS

Solomon's credentials – for writing Song of Song

It is generally accepted that the author of Song of Song was King Solomon. Consider this: from his birth, Solomon was loved by God (2 Samuel 12: 24). In fact his name was Jedidiah, which in Hebrew literally means "Beloved of the Lord" (1 Sam 12: 25).

At the beginning of Solomon's reign as the third King of Israel, God appeared to him because He loved him and knew his heart. God saw his heart when He made Himself available to Solomon by appearing in a dream and said to him "Ask! What shall I give you?" (1 Kings 3: 9 - 14).

God gave Solomon wisdom and more. It is at that time when Solomon exercised his wisdom well that Song of Solomon will have been written. We have a legacy from the wisest man at that time. He spoke three thousand proverbs and his songs were one thousand and five. He spoke of trees, from the cedar tree of Lebanon, even to the hyssop that springs out of the wall; he spoke also of animals, of birds, of creeping things and of fish (1 Kings 4: 29 - 34). In Song of Solomon we get a snapshot of one out of over a thousand songs which he wrote.

It comes from wisdom which exceeded the wisdom of all the men of the east and all the wisdom of Egypt. It speaks of intimacy and sexual relationship within the marriage union and covenant, without pollution and corruption in the marriage bond. Maybe, therefore, it holds some significant lessons to be drawn out of it for us today.

We have already mentioned the five loves. What does epithumia look like when it is working beautifully well? What does the couple relationship look like when we see eros, phileo, storge and agape present and active in the couple relationship? Let's take a look at how Solomon and the Shulamith demonstrated them in their relationship.

A study of Song of Solomon can be broken down as follows:

Chapter 1: 2 - 11	*Shulamith's first days in the palace*
Chapter 1: 12 - 14	*In a palace room*
Chapter 1: 15 to 2: 7	*In the countryside*
Chapter 2: 17	*On the way to the countryside*
Chapter 3: 1 - 5	*Shulamith waits for her fiancé*
Chapter 3: 6 - 11	*The wedding day*
Chapter 4: 1 to 5: 1	*The wedding night*
Chapter 5: 2 to 6: 3	*A problem arises*
Chapter 6: 4 - 13	*The problem resolved*
Chapter 7: 1 - 10	*In the royal bedroom*
Chapter 7: 11 to 8: 14	*In the countryside*

Despite Solomon's later credentials, God chose him to write the Song. Since it is in the Bible for a reason and purpose, we need to make sense of it.

In Song of Solomon, what we see is a marriage between the King of Israel (Solomon) and a beautiful unsophisticated, perhaps plain country girl, who the King met in the northern vineyards of his kingdom. We can call her "Shulamite" or the Shulamith. In Hebrew that is the feminine noun for "Solomon." She is otherwise nameless.

The whole book expresses the events experienced by the couple. The words and emotions they express portray for all time the love life in marriage, which honours and pleases God. Therefore it is a representation of how all marriages should be. This scripture speaks very clearly on the subject of love and sexual fulfilment in marriage.

It is a book of exquisite love poetry about a king and ultimately his queen. God's plan transcends time and cultural differences. Even though events took place in around 945 BC, it still remains the world's greatest romantic literature. It is very relevant today in showing problems that can arise in marriage, principles on solving them and how to stay in love, kindle and rekindle love. It is talking about marriage, but it is also talking about Christ and his love for us (his church).

For centuries theologians did not want to accept the plane truth - that the Song of Solomon was speaking of Godly marriage between a husband and wife and, therefore, of sexual issues. The Victorians played a strong part in denying the truths contained in Song of Solomon. The 1960's was the age of shaking off the old Victorian embarrassment which was prevalent for many many years, to the extent now that sex has become a feeling, to be felt more often without any commitment or emotional commitment. It is about excess and on demand, without love and without commitment; just a bodily need and function to be met.

In the wisdom of the Holy Spirit, the book was written from the woman's viewpoint. The bride (Shulamith) expresses her longing for her husband (Solomon) in a way that reflects the reality of Genesis 3: 16 "...and thy desire shall be to thy husband.." The husband's desire is met with equal intensity.

Historical context

The Shulamith was a country girl, required by her stepbrothers to work in the vineyards and so her skin became deeply tanned. That was in contrast to the more elegant, pampered, white skinned ladies of the king's court. She felt inferior and unworthy to be Solomon's queen. What we see is her husband skillfully and lovingly building up her self-image to let her know how acceptable she is to him, just as she is. He did it, first of all, by praise in the areas where she felt most insecure.

He voiced appreciation for her physical appearance and her lovely character and did so in very specific ways, not with vague generalities.

He compared her favourably to all other women so that she could rest in the assurance that she pleased him like no other woman could. He told her that she was flawless, perfect in his eyes. He did not praise her only when they were courting or just on the wedding night. He continued to praise her in the maturity of their marriage. Wives need to be praised for their beauty. It is that which will make them beautiful.

He refrained from criticising her - even when she may have deserved it. His words were positive. His love and approval of her was not just in private. He showed publicly his adoration and respect for her. It became obvious to others that she was the most important person in his kingdom. In private, he loved her in such a way that she could give herself to him completely, withholding nothing of herself.

With praise like that, why would someone want to commit adultery with someone else? Why would sex addiction take hold? Why would sexual frustration build up to a level that becomes destructive? Why would masturbation or self-pleasuring need to continue in the couple relationship?

In a practical way, husbands can and should continue to court their wives in private and public throughout the relationship. For example, do we make excuses for not opening a car door for our wife, because we now have central locking? Do you help her to be seated at the table? Do you hold her coat for her to put on and take off? These small courtesies give honour to your wife.

Wives cannot see your mental attitude of good intentions! They must be acted upon, especially when other people are present. Do you often look at her, especially in a room or place full of other people? Do you let her see your affectionate glances? Don't be embarrassed or give up just because you do not see anybody else behaving that way toward their wife. It is not juvenile to behave in that way towards the one who is the subject of your love.

Understand that it was not all plain sailing for Solomon and Shulamith. The marriage had problems. Of course you will have differences. The test of emotional and spiritual maturity is how you work through those problems. The marriage is the place of your own healing and perfecting. Don't leave it quickly.

Shulamith had difficulties adjusting to Solomon's demanding schedule, as the king. We see one night she expected him home, but he did not arrive until late. By then she had been offended. When he came home she would not meet him.

Note how Solomon handled the situation: instead of making an issue of it, he quietly withdrew for a few hours to give her time to think things over. That is tough and challenging for a man to do. When left alone, that gave her time to deal with her negative feelings. She reflected and recognised her unreasonableness.

That is unusual. Usually when we feel offended by the other person, left alone with time to think, does not often cause us to give thought to how the other has been wronged. Rather, it is space apart when we wallow in our own self hurt. We tend not to give the other person the benefit of the doubt. A snowball effect becomes an avalanche where past reprisals surface and feed the situation with lots of past wrongs inflicted.

What Solomon did, was not to rebuke her, but to leave a sign of his love at her door - a gift of rare perfume! Since he had not behaved as an irate lover (which it would seem he had a right to do) his wife quickly realised that she was in the wrong and sought to correct her mistake.

As soon as he had withdrawn, she began to long for him and went to look for him. We see her wandering through the street asking the watchmen whether they have seen her lover. (At times there is a cross over and blurring between her dream and reality as the story develops). When they were together again her husband reassured her with words of tender love. The same meaningful choice of words he had used on the wedding night. He had forgiven her.

Wives should realise that even though their husbands are not kings - there are some things in life that are very important to them. It may be their work. Take an interest in those things. Respect what your husband does for a living and show your admiration to him for the way in which he daily sets about his work and tasks as a father, husband and man.

Shulamith respected Solomon's manly character and often expressed her admiration for him. She was thrilled by his touch at all times and became eager for his embraces. She actually let him know that. She enjoyed his company. She planned delightful times for the two of them. She stored up delights for him in new and old ways - so as to please him. These are Eros moments. She began to blossom in the security of his love.

When she first fell in love with him she said, "*My beloved is mine and I am his*" - chapter 2: 16. Her possession of him was uppermost in her mind. Later on as the relationship developed, in chapter 6: 3 what she actually says is *"I am my beloved's and my beloved is mine"*. What had changed is a reversal of the order. Now her thinking was that his possession of her was more important. It is because Solomon had fulfilled the man role that his wife had no difficulties wanting him to possess her.

Finally, in the fullness and maturity of their love, what she says in chapter 7: 10 is *"I am my beloved's and his desire is toward me"*. What had changed now is that in the fullness of time she was so focused on her husband, that she had forgotten about possessing him. She had lost herself in his love and she gloried only in his desire for her. They were now truth Friends (phileo). She had become totally wrapped up in him and had lost herself, knowing that she had lost herself in someone who would not abuse, misuse or take advantage of her.

In chapter 2: 14, Solomon says *"Let me see thy countenance, let me hear thy voice; for sweet is thy voice and thy countenance is lovely"*. What we see is a man who loves to look into his wife's eyes, who loved to talk with her and to hear what she had to say to him. Men - do we quickly get tired of listening to our wives and looking into their eyes? Do we get tired of actually listening and hearing them and pretend we are listening? Does our behaviour put them down and show lack of interest in what they have to say? We have to reverse this if we are to get the benefits of a wife who wants to be fully absorbed in her husband so that the two becomes one in totality and are best phileo friends in love.

Becoming one is not to lose your individuality and identity. That "oneness" spoken of in Genesis can in fact be a scary thought and prospect for some. Wives - are you scared that such a oneness will cause you to lose your own identity?

Discuss those fears with your husband or another mature Christian.

The romance (Eros) of the marriage increased over the years. Let us remind ourselves of Proverbs 5: 18 - 19 *"Rejoice in the wife of your youth. As a loving hind and a graceful doe, let her breasts satisfy you at all times; be exhilarated always with her love"*.

Our study of Song of Solomon (and use different versions) will reveal the ways the couple built their love for each other. You will see the physical caressing that was all-important. Notice the delicacy of the couple's language of love.

A high point of Song of Solomon is in Chapter 4, the wedding night of the bride and groom. The first verse of Chapter 5 then contains the joyous words of the husband after their lovemaking!! *"I have come into my garden, my sister, my bride; I have gathered my myrrh along with my balsam. I have eaten my honeycomb with my honey; I have drunk my wine with my milk"*.

The verse is saying exactly what you think it is saying. It is sexual, without any apology. The young husband is describing his feelings after lovemaking. He describes love as a beautiful garden and as a wonderful feast of which he has celebrated.

Later on we then hear another voice speaking. What other person could be with the couple during their very intimate time? It is God himself, the creator looking down with total approval and affirmation of the sexual intercourse that is being shared by the married couple.

"He takes pleasure in what has taken place. He is glad they have drunk deeply of the fountain of love. Two of His own have experienced love in all the beauty and fervour and purity that he intended". See chapter 5: 1b.

Indeed, he tells them to continue to enjoy the feast of love that he has prepared. In Song of Solomon we have an inspired pattern for our own love lives.

Chapter 16

The five loves demonstrated by the couple (part 1)

In this chapter we look at the way in which the five loves are demonstrated. (The five loves is something that I cover extensively in my book entitled "The Art of Loving").

Learn to love and then learn the art of practicing love. Learn it well and then spend a lifetime in discipline, maintaining and perfecting it as your love affair progresses. Men may not need to hear the words *"I love you"* as often as women, but for sure they need to know they are valued and respected and they receive them from demonstrable acts and voice of appreciation. Men, do not refrain from using those words *"I love you"* for long, even when there is plenty of flower giving, taking out and sex! Be warned: do not make it conditional upon you being in a good mood and good place with your wife at that particular moment. Just do it!

We know that the English word *love* is much overused. We use it as much for loving a meal as we do for loving our partner, the pet or ice cream. Using one word in that manner is a recipe for misunderstanding and certainly lacks precision in what we are trying to express.

We can compare that to the way the word love is broken down and used in the Greek language. Historically the Greek language used at least five words precisely and quite distinctly to describe the various facets of love.

By looking at each of those different word descriptions, we can build up the identifying features of all the components that the word *love* should contain and be demonstrated in all healthy, progressive and fulfilling relationships. Those five words for love are **epithumia, eros, phileo, storge** and **agape**.

Every couple's love life should have all five facets of these aspects of love. Each builds on the other; each has its own special and significant place; each is distinct but inter-related and overlaps; each reinforces the other. Don't forget that! Let's look at the first of those five loves:

EPITHUMIA: (The sexual love)

Epithumia is a strong desire - of any kind. As a strong desire it can be sometimes good and sometimes bad. It is a longing for something or someone; it is to set one's heart or desire upon. Therefore, it can be viewed as having components of coveting and to lust after. We only come across the word lust as a negative expression. This is one instance when it can be used positively. It is a strong lustful and physical sexual desire in the context of a married man and woman relationship, one toward the other. Therefore, in the relationship, both husband and wife should have a strong physical desire for each other that goes on to express itself in pleasurable, sexual love making.

In Genesis 2, God created man and we see the creation of each living creature passing before Adam as a part of his job – which was to name each one. Adam will have looked at each and no doubt looked with an eager eye to see whether one of them looked like a suitable companion for him! Not such a wild thought. Remember that woman had not yet been created and so Adam had no concept of her and what a partner for man might look like.

God Himself observed that even though Adam had union with Him and sin had not yet entered creation, Adam was lonely. God said in Genesis 2: 18 *"…it is not good that man should be alone…"*. God's perfect answer was to create woman.

God took a rib out of man; woman came out of man. Little wonder then that sex that creates that closest oneness between a man and a woman is what they are constantly striving to recreate. Yes, it is a natural instinct and desire, but God put some boundaries and conditions in place for its expression.

In the beginning was the Word and the Word was with God. The three in one existed from the beginning. When God created man, He created a bipartite being, since woman was already inside man. The Word was. The Son was, as was the Spirit – in the Father. Woman was in man. The son was made flesh. God took woman out of man to give her individuality, but she remained a part of him (man) and so it is natural to want to reunite with man and get back to a place from which she came!

Sexual intercourse is the deepest express of that reunion. But the union will never be perfect. The union between God and man will be perfected in the resurrection.

When the one man and one woman became one flesh, there is a joining of two bodies physically (usually on the wedding night), but their soul and spirit were knit together before then - when the marriage vows were shared or, more accurately, at the point when each resolved in their heart that you are for me and I am for you **for life**.

The sexual response cycle

There is a difference between male and female in the way their bodies behave and react to sexual stimulation leading to sexual intercourse. It is important to understand those differences. The sexual response cycle explains those differences. Below is a graph that illustrates that difference. These are the changes that occur during sexual arousal as a response to sexual stimulation of any kind.

Fig 3

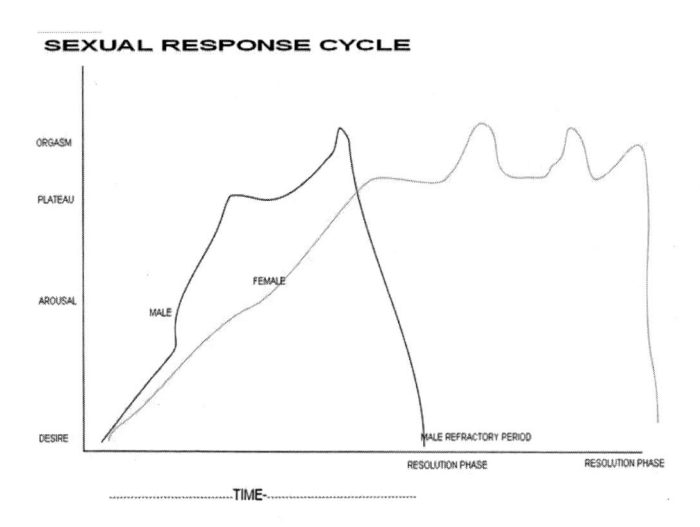

SEXUAL RESPONSE CYCLE

[Graph showing male and female sexual response curves over time, with y-axis labeled DESIRE, AROUSAL, PLATEAU, ORGASM and x-axis labeled TIME. Curves labeled MALE and FEMALE. Annotations: MALE REFRACTORY PERIOD, RESOLUTION PHASE, RESOLUTION PHASE.]

Much is attributed to Masters and Johnson for their work on sexual responses in both men and women. Masters and Johnson acknowledge the contribution provided by the earlier work of Kinsey and others. Some time later, Kaplan identified a first phase that applies to women – that of *Desire*. Desire applies only to women. Men do not need desire.

The sexual response cycle starts with *Desire* (for the woman) leading to *excitement*, *plateau*, *orgasm* and *resolution* phases. Desire is subjective and not measurable, unlike the other phases. It has qualities that represent the emotional states of hunger and wanting food. Others view it as sexual interest or libido. Studies show clearly that a poor relationship with a partner does predict low sexual desire. Where anxiety lives, desire will remain inhibited. Some women have responsive, rather than spontaneous Desire. In other words they respond to stimuli such as touch.

The second phase of Excitement represents mostly changes such as increased flow of blood to the genital organs and other blood vessels causing engorgement and lubrication. As Excitement intensifies the second phase or Plateau of high sexual arousal or tension results in a leveling off of arousal and immediately precedes the threshold level of arousal necessary to trigger Orgasm. In other words, Plateau is a period of leveling off where Excitement is no longer building for a while. Continued stimulation, however, results in a refreshed building of further Excitement that beckons in the third stage of Orgasm. Orgasm is where involuntary release of sexual tension occurs in a pleasurable rhythmic pattern and then dissipation of sexual tension.

During the fourth stage of Resolution, the anatomical and physiological changes start to dissipate and return to their normal unaroused state, contributing to a feeling of relaxation and well-being. This is an important phase for completing the full sexual response cycle of sexual intercourse and is a time when a couple can share their feelings for each other through the experience of a unique sense of closeness, promoted by a sense of relaxation and relaxed muscle tone.

It is a time of bonding and re-bonding between the couple with something Spiritual having just taken place. It is the height of the oneness. Don't break the bond of closeness too quickly by rushing to the bathroom to clean up. Sex is messy!

The duration of the phases differ between men and women. Typically, the duration of the Excitement phase is longer for women and is a very important phase for ensuring sufficient vaginal lubrication before attempts by the penis to enter the vagina without causing pain. There is much more that could be said about each phase and more is said in an earlier chapter.

Another notable difference between males and females is a *Refractory period* for males. That means after one ejaculation there is a period when males are unable to experience another ejaculation or orgasm. The length of that period depends very much upon factors which include age, desire and the effects of alcohol or medication. Women have the potential to have repeated orgasms one after the other without any Refractory period. They are multi-orgasmic. That is illustrated in the graph where the Plateau phase is again experienced, followed by Orgasm – which can be repeated over and over again, but remember ladies, all things in moderation! And here I jest only! Enjoy the capacity with which you have been equipped.

Some women have not and do not achieve an orgasm. Many do not seek multi-orgasms. Sex therapy has the very real potential to change that if the couple desire change in any aspects of a woman's orgasmic potential. Some women do squirt and ejaculate a substance that many believe to be urine. It may be urine at times, but mostly it will be a substance from the female prostate called Prostate-specific antigen which can make the Orgasm excruciatingly more pleasurable for many women who do squirt. Do not be embarrassed. Sex is messy!

The graph illustrates that women generally require more foreplay for a longer period than men. Foreplay starts before the couple gets home. It is the phone call or text message at work. It is the note found in a coat pocket with expressions of endearment.

Solomon shows us how by his use of language in Chapter 4: 1 - 16. Observe how he starts from the top of her head and works down her body very purposefully as he draws out sexual comparisons which endear his bride to him by the use of language and imagery.

The language is subtle. In verse 12 for example, it may be that the enclosed garden is very much a description of her sacred and secret place – her vagina – like a spring shut up; a fountain sealed. When opened up it gives forth a fragrance; verse 13, fragrant henna with spikenard; and verse 15, a well of living water. It indeed holds the fruits of the wound – which is representative of life.

In chapter 7: 1 - 9, he starts from the feet upwards to the head. To view his wife in this way means he must be lusting after her. He is stripping her in his mind; he is letting his fantasy have full rein; and he is entitled to do so because they are married. If they were not married, he would be sinning by committing adultery – simply by his thoughts.

By now, and in the fullness of time, he knows her anatomy well and that which it holds and gives forth. He describes her navel and the curves of her thighs. They are very intimate places. He must have permission in order to go up to the palm tree (her stature) and take hold of its branches. He will take hold of the clusters on the vine – her breasts. This is unmistakably and uncompromisingly sexual, but represented in the God endorsed manner – the relationship between husband and wife.

The fragrance of her breath means he must be up close! The roof of her mouth suggests that he must have tasted of its content in order to compare it to best wine! Something goes down smoothly when it is swallowed by the intoxicated drowsy lovers. Little wonder since in ancient times the fruit of the mandrake mentioned in verse 13 was an aphrodisiac, with narcotic properties. It was able to increase human fertility or aid in conception. In Genesis 30: 14, we observe Leah exchanging mandrakes with Rachel for a night of sleeping with their husband – Jacob.

Chapter 7: 11 - 13 portrays a picture of the couple needing to test to see whether the young bride is ready for love to be stirred and awaken; *"..let us see if the vine has budded…whether the grape blossoms are open…the pomegranates are in bloom"*.

If we look at just one of those metaphors – we will know when the pomegranate tree has now reached fruit-bearing maturity because it will drop its flowers. When the fruit has reached full colour, it can be picked and opened up. It will present an amazing sight of numerous ruby-coloured seeds and juice inside as a demonstration of ripeness. So will the Shulamith's sexuality when it is ready. Until then the stern warning in Chapter 8: 4 is to be heeded. *"Do not stir up nor awaken love until it pleases"*.

Lilies are portrayed repeatedly throughout the chapters. In chapter 1: 7, the inquisitive wife wants to know more about her husband's whereabouts, presumably so that she can go to him. By chapter 6: 3, she knows where – among the lilies. In chapter 2: 2, he uses the metaphor of her as being a lily among thorns, endorsing her statement in chapter 2: 1 that she is the lily of the valley**s**. Effectively saying to him, when you feed, you feed on me.

Chapter 2: 16 *"He feeds his flock among the lilies"*. He feeds all night (see Chapter 2: 17) as he feeds among the lilies in **his** garden to gather **his** lilies. His lips become lilies (chapter 5: 13). He clearly knows her belly (waist) area very well, since his descriptions are not confined to contours and shape. He compares them to a heap of wheat set about with lilies. He must have seen and knows well her navel - (Chapter 7: 2).

The same word for lilies is used (and there are many varieties of lilies) as is found in the title of Psalm 45: "To the Glories of the Messiah and His Bride. *To the Chief Musician. Set to "The lilies". A Contemplation of the sons of Korah. A Song of Love".*

The Shulamith returns the metaphor about her husband lover also having lips that are lilies and drip with liquid myrrh in chapter 5: 13. Remember where else there is a portrayal of liquid myrrh - when she became aroused as her lover stood at her door and wanted entrance, which she unreasonably refused; she then changed her mind as she became aroused and her fingers dripped with liquid myrrh (Chapter 5: 5). After lovemaking, the husband speaks of having gathered his myrrh – (for whom it was intended).

A bundle of myrrh might suggest "multiple" and if he lay between her breasts "all night (feasting) at his table, her spikenard sends forth its fragrance". Is this something to do with multiples of pleasure expressions between the couple? The possessive husband wants all of her and him alone.

Liquid myrrh speaks of an orgasmic build up. Maybe the French words *la petite mort* is an apt description meaning the *"little death"*; describing the spiritual release that comes with orgasm. Myrrh is symbolic of post death embalming as we see in John 19: 39. Maybe this is not all so far fetch – for look at what the lover says about his love encounter experience with the Shulamith in Chapter 8: 6 "…for love is as strong as death, Jealousy as cruel as the grave…". Love is compared to death. The two are intricately woven and intertwined. If one hurt, the other hurt. They are one. Jealousy out of control is awesomely powerful and destructive. A most vehement flame (chapter 8: 6).

In chapter 7: 9, the Shulamith continues with Solomon's metaphor of quality wine and encourages his endearments. It is intoxicating such that she feels it herself even as they embrace leading to sleep. She gives herself to him freely. Lovemaking tightens the bond between the two. Solomon is set as a seal upon her heart and arm. His left hand under her head in an embrace is very much a lover's position portrayed in chapter 2: 6.

Chapter 7: 11 - 12 shows the progress from foreplay to the developing height of sexual tension. Young lovers are in the habit of waking early and yielding to their passion. She talks about checking on progress. See if the vine has budded; whether the grape blossom is a metaphor for heightened sexual arousal. When all is in blossom and ready, she will give herself to him. He may enter her.

The flow of her love juices is an indication of readiness. She is in bloom and the grape blossoms are open; she will give him her love. In Verse 13, their passion gives off fragrance. Lovers know each other's sexual odour. It is a tonic that comes out of the scent of love juices. Their union gives off such a strong odour.

Chapter 17

The five loves demonstrated by the couple (part 2)

Sex can be used to punish, frustrate, reject or pay back. It can be turned off deliberately, purposefully and by choice. The quiet treatment, criticism, suspicion, anger, hurt, silence, misunderstanding, fear, hostility or guilt can have their tentacles in the relationship. They will be hindrances that play a part in shutting down certain stages in the sexual responses. Anxiety, self-consciousness, scoring and performance pressures are other attitudes and behaviours that will affect the phases in the sexual response cycle.

Sex therapists are assisted in their work by having a good understanding of predisposing, precipitating and maintaining factors, which are psychological causes of sexual dysfunction. The dysfunctions include lack of orgasm by either party; pain during penetrative sex; male erectile difficulties; inability to allow the penis into the vagina; premature ejaculation, lack of desire or interest in sex.

Predisposing factors from early childhood experiences may arise from overt or covert messages about sex. They may arise because of a restrictive upbringing, perception about the quality of relationships between parents, inadequate sexual information and traumatic early sexual experiences (of which childhood sexual abuse is a key factor). Also, early insecurity in own psychosexual role, such as lack of comfort with personal sexuality and, therefore, an adverse view about sexual identity, masturbation, own body development, as well as other people's view of self – all can contribute to sexual disorders (now called dysfunctions).

Precipitants are events, circumstances and situations associated with and connected to the sexual problem. When certain circumstances are recognised as being present, they act as a precipitant to the problem reoccurring. Precipitants may be physical or psychological; they restrict the sexual response.

Precipitants include loss of interest by a woman following childbirth; discord in the general relationship (which may also then become a maintaining factor); cheating - such as an affair or other guilt and secrets; unreasonable expectations (where things such as inability to achieve multiple orgasms, not "coming" together and sexual myths are active).

One partner may suffer random failure, of which stress, alcohol, medication and drugs are contributors. Reaction to organic factors such as a heart attack or hysterectomy, ageing and issues around physiological changes from ageing, depression and anxiety, as well as other traumatic sexual experiences (such as rape and unwanted pregnancy) - are precipitants.

Maintaining factors are those things that are actually present and explain why the problem continues. It may be performance anxiety, which will inhibit the natural sexual response cycle.

Hand in hand with anxiety is anticipation of failure, which may lead to guilt. Loss of attraction between the partners, poor communication, discord in the general relationship, impaired or poor self image, inadequate sexual information, lack of knowledge and sexual myths (which are also precipitants) - are also maintainers. Alongside are such things as insufficient foreplay, psychiatric disorders and alcoholism.

I single out the fear of intimacy for further mention because fear of prolonged intimacy may cause avoidance or limited contact between the couple in case it leads further than one of them wants. They desire affection and contact, especially when sex is not working well for them. Yet contact is avoided and limited so as to regulate the frequency of attempting to have sexual intercourse, which evokes such strong memories of failure. A lose/lose dilemma and a spiraling vicious circle is established.

The need for sex therapy is readily identifiable in all of the scenarios above. The benefits of sex therapy are available to the elderly who want an active sex life, as well as those who suffer from various disabilities and so often are not well catered for by other services. They so often require help, but

GPs and other medics are not always trained, familiar or comfortable with the subject matter in order to even raise it and sign post the elderly and disabled to those that can help.

Correct knowledge is a starting point. There may be misconceptions, misinformation, false teachings, wrong views - all of which may have to be challenged, discarded and right thinking replace them, based on correct information. Understand that you can turn off your interest in sex and can turn off (at least) the capacity for sex.

Why not try one of the positions shown to us by Solomon and his bride in Song of Solomon 2: 6 and again in Chapter 8: 3. The man positions his hand under his wife's head and the right hand is free to embrace her or do other things! Little wonder that each time that we see this pose, it comes with a warning to the virgins not to stir up or awaken love until it pleases – in chapter 8: 4 and chapter 2: 7.

A healthy sexual life requires the development and maintaining a lifetime love affair. Even if you already have a good relationship, it can be better! You have a right to expect and anticipate increased sexual pleasure year after year. You have no right to expect diminished sexual pleasure. Diminished sexual pleasure need not come with older age and certainly need not take up residence being as the norm. In middle age and senior years, sensitive, uninhibited practiced lovemaking can become exhilarating with a partner who responds and performs in a complementary way.

We have been left with a very bad image of sex and a legacy throughout history and particularly from the Victorian age. Some will witness to the fact that they knew little about sex and later realised how much their parents' disapproval and negative images have left a negative impression upon them. It may take years to let go of and give yourself permission to embrace and enjoy sex.

Many learned about sex from what they picked up from magazines, library books or school kids' talk. Sexual myths became entrenched and were believed and practiced for a long time. Maybe even now those sexual myths are still being practiced!

We must love our spouse's body as our own. We would not hurt our own body. Therefore unreasonable demands are, of course, not acceptable, since we would not do anything to hurt one's own body. Having unreasonable sexual demands is to try to hurt our own body and the other person. What is an unreasonable demand? That is something for the couple to discuss and negotiate, but always with an eye on the fact that we must not do harm to ourselves or others – physically, emotionally, sexually or otherwise. We should be doing battle to see who can be the better servant to the other.

Sex without signs of love is sure to create resentment, not response. Prepare the ground for lovemaking long before the sexual act itself takes place. Use affectionate pats, text messages and other ways to endear you to your partner. Admiring glances across the crowded room makes the person feel and know they are special. These acts are foreplay. They commence before getting home!

Once you are together you should shut out the world. Ensure complete privacy, particularly from children. Use a lock if it will aid relaxation for one more than the other. Fear of being caught in the act is an inhibitor for many. It does affect the sexual response cycle.

Don't take the sexual relationship so seriously. Don't aim for simultaneous orgasm on every occasion. Keep sex light-hearted and fun. It should be recreational; especially so, since it is suppose to be regular (habitual) and for a lifetime! If it is hard work, then sooner or later it will diminish. Initially it probably will be an effort, but as you work at it, it should become recreational pleasure. Recreational pleasure does not have to mean routine, predictable and repetitive.

Women do not always need or desire an orgasm during sexual intercourse. Husbands find that hard to understand because they view it from their male bodily response and expectation. "Did the earth move for you?" is an intimidating question to ask the other person just after lovemaking. What can they say?

– especially if the earth did not move! Men are guilty of asking the question too frequently and at the wrong time. Wait until a different occasion if it has to be asked - because it was not witnessed! Begin to learn about your wife's reactions during the sexual response phases and soon you will not need to ask!

Vicious cycles can be created within relationships and maintained for many years. A wife feels a failure because she cannot work up the right physical response leading to an orgasm. She tries harder. As she tries harder, the more the natural reflex action required for an orgasm fades. She begins to sense her husband's disapproval or disappointment and the sex act becomes increasingly painful physically and emotionally.

She begins to avoid sex. If her husband persists, she feels used. Resentment sets in. A low self-image may begin to appear and soon she begins to think that her husband only has ulterior motives when he is being nice to her. Our mouth betrays us with words that slip out and we did not even know that such levels of resentment had built up inside our hearts.

The husband's confidence may become shaken by the sense of failure at not being able to bring sexual release to his wife. As his wife begins to avoid sex, he may get the feeling that she is no longer interested in him. He begins to wonder if she even loves him. They are on a downward spiral. A vicious circle has set in. The stage is set for dysfunctions.

We employ fight, flight or freeze when core emotional needs are not being met. We all have these needs and they have to be kept topped up. They are such things as feeling respected, valued, secure, appreciated and others. We fight, flight or freeze to get those needs met, but we may be seeking too much from each other. Those needs have to be met by many others and from different circles in which we interact. Low core emotional needs place both parties in a vulnerable situation; vulnerable to affairs and other attractions which feed those needs.

Remember, orgasms happen in the brain not the genitals and so the focus of our attention can be the very thing which disrupts and hinders orgasm. Barriers build up from persistent discouragement. The sense of rejection, inadequacy and failure needs to be broken.

The couple will need to turn away from concentration on sexual climax and the problems of sex and relearn how to enjoy each other without the pressures of sexual intercourse. Ban sexual intercourse for a period. Stick to it and use the same amount of time to explore each other's bodies without sexual intercourse. Only you stand between your situation and the solution.

EROS: (Romance)

The second of our five loves is Eros. The word has been corrupted by the English word "erotic". Eros is the driver for the romance in the relationship. Sometimes sensual, it is the idea, desire and feeling of wanting to be together and yearning to unite; to possess the other, such is the intensity of the feelings.

Eros is romantic, passionate and sentimental. It is so readily visible in the early days of the developing relationship. It is the driver that causes lovers to write love poetry, love notes and give pet names to each other – like piggy wiggy! The impulse to miss the train or bus easily wins, even though it is pouring with rain because a small gift is spotted in a shop window that you desire to buy. The radiant smile of the receiver makes the detour so worthwhile.

STORGE: (Security)

Storge is the third of our five loves. It is a most valuable and expensive gift. It is described as the kind of love shared by parents and children, brothers and sisters; a relationship which will always be there for you, despite being rejected by others; a safe place/haven.

It is the need (which we all have) to belong or to be a part of a close-knit system with people who care, are loyal and sincere. It is a relationship that provides emotional refuge from a world which can be cold, harsh, hard and uncompromisingly hostile. Storge provides the atmosphere of security in which love is able to dwell, thrive and flourish.

PHILEO: (Fellowship/Friendship)

Phileo is the fourth of our five loves. It is the love one feels for a cherished friend of either sex. This love is conditional and is reactive to what it sees in the other and what comes back. It is a love that cherishes and has tender affection for the beloved, but always expects a response. (This is in stark contrast to agape that we shall see does not demand a response).

Phileo is a comradeship, sharing, communication and friendship. It is dear friends who enjoy each other's closeness and companionship; sharing each other's intimate thoughts, feelings, attitudes, plans, dreams, time, interests, aspirations, as well as intimate things that would not be shared with anyone else.

Sol 5: 16 commends us to have that Phileo best friend: *"This is my beloved, and this is my friend."*

AGAPE: (Unconditional)

Agape is the fifth of our five loves. At some point in a relationship we may be tested harshly indeed by a crisis: pinches and crunches happen in all relationships. They can jolt and further disrupt the harmony of a marriage. They are the little foxes which the Shulamith warned about in Sol 2: 15.

Perhaps for a longer period than we could have imagined or expected we have tried to love the unlovable. We are face-to-face with the stark reality that this is a marriage *"for better or for worse"*. That is what we not only promised, but covenanted to honour. Do we live up to the promise and covenant when the going gets very tough indeed.

Unlovable traits show up in the partner. The toll on you has already been great. Yet the need in them will only be met by you continuing to express and demonstrate unconditional love. A very tall order indeed. It is just not sustainable by a good dose of will power. Will power will fade on a bad day when you have given repeatedly into the relationship, but nothing seems to be coming back from the other. You need the Holy Spirit in order to sustain Agape unconditional loving. Recognise that well! A small, but close supportive group of family and friends will also be essential. The going does get very tough, but the potential reward of winning your partner back into the relationship will make it worth it. You, the Holy Spirit and 10,000 angels at your disposal make you a majority.

More happenings between the couple

In Sol Chapter 1: 2 - 4, there is a steamy bedroom scene. The Shulamith hungers for her husband's kisses. Not just a peck will do. She longs to feel his deep kiss inside her mouth. She wants kisses which take her breath away. Solomon has an erotic scent of perfume oils on his body. She becomes even more bold and enticing in her invitation and begs him to seize her and race with her to the seclusion of their bedchamber. She wants him now and is forceful about it!

Observe in Chapter 1: 14 mention of En Gedi (a place). It was a lush, verdant oasis formed by a hidden spring which poured forth from limestone rock at the top of a cliff. Cool water tumbled down forming a tropical paradise filled with soaring birds and exotic plants. En Gedi was, therefore, a romantic place where the sweet scent of henna blossoms filled the air.

The Shulamith is telling her husband that he is an oasis; her own personal En Gedi; a hideaway where lovers can discover sexual refreshment. En Gedi can be lived out in the bedroom (or in the car parked in the garage!) and recreated by lovers who desire to do so. The bedroom can become a place of beauty and rest because of what the couple do to transform it with very little expense and some creativity. The sex therapist shows and encourages the couple to do just that as they embark upon their sensate focus work.

Words and expressions of praise are Shulamith's love language and we see her need of then at the end of Chapter 1. They trade endearments and sexual compliments, which continue into Chapter 2: 1 - 6. She comments upon the luxurious couch, beautiful canopy and about Solomon's thoughtfulness in constructing the bridal chamber.

They compare each other to flowers and fruits. She praises him above all other men and as a lover. Passion is mounting. They are actively involved in love play.

In literature of that era "fruit" was often equated with the male genitals or with semen when used in the context that the Shulamith does. Fruit is also characteristic of the female body parts, such as her breasts and genitals.

We see a further example of that in chapter 7: 7 – 8, when referring to her as a palm tree and her breasts as being like its clusters. Fruit tends to be put into the mouth! This is the peak of love play and foreplay with intense mounting arousal.

Listen to her unashamed active participation as she encourages him. *"Let us see if the vine has budded…"* (Chapter 7: 12). Song of Solomon is undoubtedly sexual in every way. The delicacy of the sexual language has examples of Eros throughout the Book.

What can women learn about this business?

John 8:32 reminds us that it is the truth that we know (and actively practice) which will set us free. We must, however, read the previous verse 31, because there is a condition. It is the truth that we consistently practice and apply and that truth will then set us free because of the promise in verse 32.

Here are some truths that can help us in the scenario of sexual relationships. In Titus 2: 3 there is a commendation to older women in the church to be a good example and to teach the younger women good things, including to express love to their husbands *"that the word of God may not be blasphemed"*. It sits well with the commendation in Song of Solomon 1: 8 that *"If you do not know…Follow in the footsteps of the flock, [A]nd feed your goats beside the shepherds' tent"*. It is time that our older ladies took their rightful place. Yet, maybe, they too are from a generation that were not well served by the church in this subject matter and, therefore, do not feel equipped to fulfil the Titus commendation.

Compare that to the admonition which we see in Chapter 2: 15 where the little foxes (as small scavengers) can get in and spoil the vines – the root of the relationship – gnawing at its root and disrupting harmony. Lack of caring for the relationship, coasting and taking each other for granted can cause such lapses to have major repercussion where no one is heeding the signs of conflict mounting.

Errors in judgment can be costly. We see the Shulamith make an error of judgment that she later regrets. Young and tempestuous toward her beloved in the early days of courtship, she questions her obligations in chapter 1: 7. It is interesting that she faces the very same issue in chapter 5: 7. Although this depicts her dream, the watchmen disrespect her by pulling her veil away from her; the very same garment that she questioned as needing to wear in the midst of her beloved's companions.

She had refused to open the door to her lover when he wanted entrance to her bedroom, because it was now late. She was offended because his work had delayed him coming to her. Her uses petty excuses as to why she cannot get up to open the door. She had bathed. She was not presentable. She would have to put on the right attire. Even she was not convinced by her own reasoning, so when he had gone and she was left to her own thoughts, she quickly regretted her stance. She had actually become aroused by her lovers persistence. She found herself running through the streets trying to find her lover, risking abuse by the watchmen who saw her.

What men can learn about loving their wives

Song of Solomon shows us an example of Ephesians 5 in action; that teaching on "submission", which husbands throw at wives and wives back to husbands with equal counter attack. What I say is that whenever a man uses Ephesians 5: 22 – 33, then it is clear evidence that he has not played his rightful role in the application of that passage. It starts with the man – all the time! If he had got his part right, he would have no difficulty seeing the Ephesians 5 wife in his midst! There is a high price for getting it wrong.

Could it be that the desires of your heart are not being met, because your prayers are being hindered? Remember that the two have become one. Could the hindrance be that told to us in 1 Peter 3: 7? If we (the righteous) are not treating each other with honour, kindness and respect, then we restrict His righteousness to flow through us and we experience hindered prayers.

What does hindered prayers look like?

It is clearly identified and explained to us in 1 Peter 3: 7: husbands, the commandment is to you. Dwell with your wife with understanding, giving honour, as to the weaker vessel and as being heirs together (recognising your oneness) of the grace of life, that your prayers may not be hindered.

The prayers of a righteous person is powerful and avails much, but if we are not treating others with honour, kindness and respect, then we put hindrances on His ability to operate in us. We must treat each other with understanding such that we consider their needs above our own.

When we do not treat others with dignity, kindness, humility and with a humble heart, then we should quickly seek forgiveness – which removes the hindrance to our prayers. Remember *"…and forgive us our trespasses as we forgive those that trespass against us."*

There is a condition precedent that we must first fulfil. We are not victims or hostages to circumstances. We do have choice. We may and can choose not to exercise choice to forgive. We can pretend to plan to intend to do the right thing! And genuinely believe in our intention! But action does at times speak louder than words. Time soon tells whether our good intention was acted upon.

Daniel experienced hindrance to his prayers. Not because he had unforgiven sin, but because the children of God have an enemy and those who do his bidding block and delay those who have the answer released to us by our God. In Daniel 9: 16-19 we see Daniel praying. We see swift answer coming from Gabriel in Daniel 9: 20 - 23.

Later on, and in another situation, we see something rather different in Daniel 10: 11 - 13. On this occasion, of his prayers in Daniel 10: 11 - 13, we hear that Daniel's prayers were heard immediately and the answer released, but the Prince of Persian (Satan) withstood the Angel (who bore the answer). Interestingly enough, the Angel needed help from Michael in order to overcome and break the hold. Our Heavenly Father sends help to us to unblock the answers to our prayers. Heed the help even though it takes the form of another person who comes to show us truth.

Many are in leadership roles and so often neglect their own vineyard – which represents our family members and home life wellbeing. It can be said of them – as in Song of Solomon 1: 6 *"…They have made me the keeper of the vineyards…but my own vineyard I have not kept"*.

Aspects of the prodigal son's personality have admirable qualities. Here is someone who made some wrong choices from bad decisions and was on a destructive course. He was, however, able to see his errors, change his mind and turn around. That must always be an admirable quality. Fewer people have the resolve to follow through a decision to turn around. He did and to his credit he was restored.

Take warning from Hebrews 4: 2 *"for indeed the gospel was preached to us as well as to them; but the word which they heard did not profit them, not being mixed with faith in those who heard it"*.

Epilogue

The great unseen love story between Jacob, Rachel and Leah

…but not as you first thought!

In this often unappreciated love story of love stories, we see the tangible reward which consistent demonstration of the five loves - epithumia, eros, phileo, storge and agape love at work - can deliver in the relationship between a husband and a wife.

Not loved, want love, desire love, lost love, first love, broken love – love restoration; it is possible, even when the years have taken a toll and experiencing it again, seems to be unachievable.

Who was Jacob's favourite wife? Leah or Rachel?

Genesis 29:16 - 20 (NKJV)

16 Now Laban had two daughters: the name of the elder was Leah, and the name of the younger was Rachel. 17 Leah's eyes were delicate, but Rachel was beautiful of form and appearance.

18 Now Jacob loved Rachel; so he said, "I will serve you seven years for Rachel your younger daughter."

19 And Laban said, "It is better that I give her to you than that I should give her to another man. Stay with me." 20 So Jacob served seven years for Rachel, and they seemed only a few days to him because of the love he had for her.

Genesis 29:23 - 26 (NKJV)

23 Now it came to pass in the evening, that he took Leah his daughter and brought her to Jacob; and he went in to her. 24 And Laban gave his maid Zilpah to his daughter Leah as a maid. 25 So it came to pass in the morning, that behold, it was Leah. And he said to Laban, "What is this you have done to me? Was it not for Rachel that I served you? Why then have you deceived me?"

26 And Laban said, "It must not be done so in our country, to give the younger before the firstborn.

Genesis 29:28-29 (NKJV)

28 Then Jacob did so and fulfilled her week. So he gave him his daughter Rachel as wife also. 29 And Laban gave his maid Bilhah to his daughter Rachel as a maid.

Genesis 29:30-35 (NKJV)

30 Then Jacob also went in to Rachel, and he also loved Rachel more than Leah. And he served with Laban still another seven years.

31 When the Lord saw that Leah was unloved, He opened her womb; but Rachel was barren.

32 So Leah conceived and bore a son, and she called his name Reuben;[a] for she said, "The Lord has surely looked on my affliction. Now therefore, my husband will love me."

33 Then she conceived again and bore a son, and said, "Because the Lord has heard that I am unloved, He has therefore given me this son also." And she called his name Simeon.

34 She conceived again and bore a son, and said, "Now this time my husband will become attached to me, because I have borne him three sons." Therefore, his name was called Levi.

35 And she conceived again and bore a son, and said, "Now I will praise the Lord." Therefore, she called his name Judah. Then, she stopped bearing.

Let us now jump forward to when Jacob and Esau met again in Genesis 33:1-3 (NKJV)

33 Now Jacob lifted his eyes and looked, and there, Esau was coming, and with him were four hundred men. So he divided the children among Leah, Rachel, and the two maidservants. 2 And he put the maidservants and their children in front, Leah and her children behind, and Rachel and Joseph last. 3 Then he crossed over before them and bowed himself to the ground seven times, until he came near to his brother.

So which one of these two wives do you think Jacob loves more – Leah or Rachel? Even though Leah could see that Jacob's eyes were for Rachel more than for her, there is no doubt of her strong love for him. "Tender eyed" and, therefore, probably weak eyed from birth or lacked luster, would not have been a pleasing and attractive attribute. Leah had a visible disadvantage to her rival. Rachel was described as "beautiful and well-favoured". Yet, it is quite clear that Leah absolutely and genuinely loved Jacob and God favoured her.

We see the way in which God remembered her, opened her wound and she became the mother of six of the twelve tribes of Israel. That is big! A very big deal!

Consider the meaning of the names of each of Leah's six sons. "Praise and honour" and "thanksgiving to God", are just some of their meanings and clearly represent her heart felt desire. It was found acceptable to Him and just maybe the God who looks at the heart, rather than outward appearance, honoured her back as being the more suited to be the instrument he used to establish the tribes of Israel.

It took longer for Jacob to get in line, but somewhere in the decades of their lives together, he did; he found greater favour and love for Leah!

Now let's jump forward to Rachel's death in Genesis 35:17-23 (NKJV)

> *17 Now it came to pass, when she was in hard labor, that the midwife said to her, "Do not fear; you will have this son also." 18 And so it was, as her soul was departing (for she died), that she called his name Ben-Oni;[a] but his father called him Benjamin.[b] 19 So Rachel died and was buried on the way to Ephrath (that is, Bethlehem). 20 And Jacob set a pillar on her grave, which is the pillar of Rachel's grave to this day.*

We are not told about Jacob's emotions arising from Rachel's death, but we know it must have been great. Let us move forward a lot of decades later. What do we witness at Jacobs death?

Genesis 49:29-32 (NKJV)

29 Then he charged them and said to them: "I am to be gathered to my people; bury me with my fathers in the cave that is in the field of Ephron the Hittite,

30 in the cave that is in the field of Machpelah, which is before Mamre in the land of Canaan, which Abraham bought with the field of Ephron the Hittite as a possession for a burial place.

31 There they buried Abraham and Sarah, his wife, there they buried Isaac and Rebekah, his wife, and there I buried Leah.

Between Rachel's death and Jacob's death, had something changed so that Jacob chose to be buried next to Leah instead of Rachel? It surely must have done. The fullness of time witnessed a shift in the person he most loved by the end of his life.

What insight can we gain from this portrayal of love? The ability to regain love in a marriage where it has declined is very real indeed. Consistent application, practice and demonstration of the five loves, can produce an outcome way greater than you ever thought. Restoration, refreshment, rekindle, revitalize and remove the barriers in a marriage are the rewards for those who follow God's way.

It was Leah who bore Judah (whose name means *praise*) and through his line the Saviour came – Jesus Christ, Saviour of the world.

Gary McFarlane LLM, BA, Postgrad Dip in Couple Counselling, Cert in psychosexual Therapy, Cert in Sex Addiction & Compulsivity, Cert in Couple Counselling.

Reference List

1. Nolte, D.L. In: Clarke,M., 2003. *Child Health.* Juta. p.22.

2. Waltz, W. and Waltz, L., 2006. *The Porn Trap.* New York: Penguin Books. p.25.

3. Telegraph View., 2010. A Sexual Disaster for Teenagers and Society. *The Telegraph.* [online] Available at: <http://www.telegraph.co.uk/health/7964538/A-sexual-disaster-for-teenagers-and-society.html>

4. Aitkenhead, D., 2010. *Teenage kicks - are they hooked on porn?* pp.52-59.

5. Aitkenhead, D., 2010. *Teenage kicks - are they hooked on porn?*

6. Aitkenhead, D., 2010. *Teenage kicks - are they hooked on porn?*

7. Ministry of Truth, 2012. *Are 11 Year Olds Watching Porn?* [online] Available at: <http://www.ministryoftruth.me.uk/2012/05/05/are-11-years-olds-viewing-porn/>

8. Hill, C., 2009. Study: Teens spend 87 hours per year looking at porn. *Daily News.* [online] Available at: <http://www.nydailynews.com/news/money/study-teens-spend-87-hours-year-online-porn-article-1.389603>

9. *(Aitkenhead, Teenage kicks - are they hooked on porn? pp52-59, 2010).*

10. Daily Mail Reporter, 2011. Fury as Channel 4 Teaches Youngsters Kama Sutra Positions in Graphic 'Joys of Teen Sex'. *Daily Mail.*

11. Shaw, V., 2007. UK has the Highest Teenage Pregnancy Rate in Europe. *The Independent.*

12. Bloom, S.G., no date. *Blue-Eyes, Brown-Eyes: The Experiment that Shocked the Nation and Turned a Town Against It's Most Famous Daughter.* [pdf] Available at: <http://www.uiowa.edu/~poroi/seminars/2004-5/bloom/poroi_paper.pdf> pp.3-4.

13. The Huffington Post, 2014. Short People May Experience Feelings of Inferiority, Research Suggests. *The Huffington Post.*

14. Office for National Statistics, 2009. *Households and Families.* [pdf] Available at: <http://www.ons.gov.uk/ons/rel/social-trends-rd/social-trends/social-trends-39/chapter-2.pdf> p.2.

15. Hodgson, A., 2007. *One Person Households: Opportunities for Consumer Goods Companies.* [online] Available at: <http://blog.euromonitor.com/2007/09/one-person-households-opportunities-for-consumer-goods-companies.html>

16. Pidd, H., 2009. I Don't: Marriage Rates Crash to an All Time Low. *The Guardian.*

17. Office for National Statistics, 2009. *Social Trends.* [pdf] Available at:
<https://plus.google.com/url?sa=t&rct=j&q=&esrc=s&sourc

e=web&cd=1&cad=rja&uact=8&ved=0CCAQFjAA&url=http%3A%2F%2Fwww.ons.gov.uk%2Fons%2Frel%2Fsocial-trends-rd%2Fsocial-trends%2Fsocial-trends-39%2Fsocial-trends-full-report.pdf&ei=EN25U9LOKamq0QXtqIGYAQ&usg=AFQjCNFj7pptwdx9rxAsUndNsX9mJKP3xA&sig2=a22WJsr3OO1up-xQ_PlI-A>

18. Wallop, H., 2009. Death of the Traditional Family. *The Telegraph*. [online] Available at: <http://www.telegraph.co.uk/women/mother-tongue/5160857/Death-of-the-traditional-family.html>

19. Office for National Statistics, 2013. *Statistical Bulletin: Families and Households, 2013*. [pdf] Available at: <http://www.ons.gov.uk/ons/dcp171778_332633.pdf> p.1.

20. Department for Work and Pensions, 2013. *Households Below Average Income: An Analysis of the Income Distribution 1994/95 - 2009/10*. p.108.

21. Office for National Statistics, 2013. *Statistical Bulletin: Families and Households, 2013*. [pdf] Available at: <http://www.ons.gov.uk/ons/dcp171778_332633.pdf> p.5.

22. Office for National Statistics, 2013. *Statistical Bulletin: Families and Households, 2013*. [pdf] Available at: <http://www.ons.gov.uk/ons/dcp171778_332633.pdf> p.5.

23. Office for National Statistics, 2013. *Statistical Bulletin: Families and Households, 2013*. [pdf] Available at: <http://www.ons.gov.uk/ons/dcp171778_332633.pdf> p.4.

24. Office for National Statistics, 2013. *Statistical Bulletin: Families and Households, 2013.* [pdf] Available at: <http://www.ons.gov.uk/ons/dcp171778_332633.pdf> p.4.

25. Morgan, P., 2000. *Marriage Lite: The Rise of Cohabitation and its Consequences.* [pdf] Available at: <http://www.civitas.org.uk/pdf/cs04.pdf> p.13.

26. Morgan, P., 2000. *Marriage Lite: The Rise of Cohabitation and its Consequences.* [pdf] Available at: <http://www.civitas.org.uk/pdf/cs04.pdf> p.13.

27. Morgan, P., 2000. *Marriage Lite: The Rise of Cohabitation and its Consequences.* [pdf] Available at: <http://www.civitas.org.uk/pdf/cs04.pdf> p.28.

28. Morgan, P., 2000. *Marriage Lite: The Rise of Cohabitation and its Consequences.* [pdf] Available at: <http://www.civitas.org.uk/pdf/cs04.pdf> p.vii.

29. Morgan, P., 2000. *Marriage Lite: The Rise of Cohabitation and its Consequences.* [pdf] Available at: <http://www.civitas.org.uk/pdf/cs04.pdf> p.49.

30. Morgan, P., 2000. *Marriage Lite: The Rise of Cohabitation and its Consequences.* [pdf] Available at: <http://www.civitas.org.uk/pdf/cs04.pdf> p.42.

31. Office for National Statistics, 2012. *Births and Deaths in England and Wales, 2011.* p.8.

32. Northern Ireland Statistics and Research Agency, 2012. [online] Available at: <http://www.nisra.gov.uk/demography/default.asp2.htm>

33. General Register Office for Scotland, 2013. [online] Available at: <http://www.gro-scotland.gov.uk/statistics/theme/vital-events/general/bmd-preliminary/2012.html>

34. Office for National Statistics, 2014. *Divorces in England and Wales, 2012.* p.1.

35. Evangelical Alliance, 2013. *Family Life in the UK.* [online] Available at: <http://www.eauk.org/culture/statistics/family-life-in-the-uk.cfm>

36. Evangelical Alliance, 2013. *Family Life in the UK.* [online] Available at: <http://www.eauk.org/culture/statistics/family-life-in-the-uk.cfm>

37. Office for National Statistics, 2013. *Divorces in England and Wales, 2011.* p.1.

38. Northern Ireland Statistics and Research Agency, 2012. *Marriages, Divorces and Civil Partnerships in Northern Ireland, 2011.* p.37.

39. General Register Office for Scotland, 2013. *Divorces Time Series Data.* [online] Available at: *<http://www.gro-scotland.gov.uk/statistics/theme/vital-events/divorces-and-dissolutions/time-series.html.>*

40. Evangelical Alliance, 2013. *Family Life in the UK.* [online] Available at: <http://www.eauk.org/culture/statistics/family-life-in-the-uk.cfm>

41. Office for National Statistics, 2012. *Divorces in England and Wales, 2011.* p.7.

42. Office for National Statistics, 2012. *Divorces in England and Wales, 2011.* p.7.

43. Lewis, C.S. In: The Happiness Project. *Daily Quotes.* [online] Available at: <http://www.gretchenrubin.com/daily-quotes/>

44. Nelson, P., 2012. *There's a Hole in my Sidewalk: The Romance of Self Discovery.* [ebook] Simon and Schuster.

45. Keiling, R., and Keiling, S.H., no date. *Pornography Addiction Treatment.* [online] Available at: <http://personalgrowthandcreativity.com/sex-addiction-treatment/pornography-addiction-treatment/>

46. Landry, J., 2010. *Internet Abuse Can Kill a Company: What Can You Do About It?* [pdf] Available at: <http://www.gagetelephone.com/Files/Press/TAG-Gage-AcceptablePolicies.pdf> p.1.

47. Young, K.S., and Case, C.J. 2003. *Employee Internet Abuse: Risk Management Strategies and Their Effectiveness.* [pdf] Available at: <http://netaddiction.com/articles/eia_strategies.pdf> p.1.

48. Hudson-Allez, G., 2009. *Infant Losses, Adult Searches: A Neural and Developmental Perspective on Psychopathology and Sexual Offending.* p.158.

49. Cooper, Boies, et al., 1999. In: Hudson-Allez, G., 2009. *Infant Losses, Adult Searches: A Neural and Developmental Perspective on Psychopathology and Sexual Offending.* p.159.

50. Hudson-Allez, G., 2009. *Infant Losses, Adult Searches: A Neural and Developmental Perspective on Psychopathology and Sexual Offending.* p.158.

51. Hudson-Allez, G., 2009. *Infant Losses, Adult Searches: A Neural and Developmental Perspective on Psychopathology and Sexual Offending.* p.158.

52. Hudson-Allez, G., 2009. *Infant Losses, Adult Searches: A Neural and Developmental Perspective on Psychopathology and Sexual Offending.* p.158.

53. Doring, 2000. In: Miller, V., 2011. *Understanding Digital Culture.* SAGE. p.176.

54. Shakespeare, W., 1693. *Twelfth Night.* In: Mowat, B.A. ed., 2011. *Twelfth Night.* Simon and Schuster. p.7.

55. Wood, J.T., 1974. *Poem For Everyman.* In: Rogers, A. and Horrocks, N., 2010. *Teaching Adults.* McGraw-Hill International. p.82.

Gary McFarlane *is a Relate trained and experienced Relationship Counsellor, Mediator, Sex Therapist, Sex Addiction & Love Addiction Therapist. All of which are undertaken by Skype, Facetime, other webcam utilities, telephone and face to face with clients from all parts of the country and indeed, all over the world. He is a member of the British Association of Counsellors & Psychotherapists (BACP), the Association of Christian Counsellors (ACC) and the Association for the Treatment of Sexual Addiction & Compulsivity (ATSAC). That includes working with Churches re-integrating those with sexual indiscretion, back into ministry. A list of workshops and seminars is shown below:*

Seminar/Training support from Gary McFarlane

- Managing Ministers with indiscretions, back into ministry

- Leadership skills/training: "The distinctive leader"

- Conflict management & resolution: Blessed are the peacemakers

- Effective peacemaking

- Effective confession, forgiveness and change

- The change process: Changing your mind so that you can change your life

- Leadership skills: Personality traits and Transactional Analysis (TA), masks people wear and games people play

- The 5 loves: Their application to love rebuilding, refreshing, resurrecting and rekindling relationships

- Song of Solomon: As a pattern for lovers – What we can learn and apply

- Communication and miscommunication: Improving how we do it

- A lifetime love affair: John 10: 10 – A tall order?

- Sexual knowledge for enhancing sex in marriage

- Addiction: Love & sex addiction

- When love don't live here anymore

- Overcoming sexual temptation

- Singleness and their issues

- Effective Hearing and Listening skills

- Ministers symposium: Sexual issues affecting our churches - Our response

- Diagnosing the fitness of your marriage

- Fundamental Biblical truths about marriage

- What is sex addiction? What is love addiction?

- What is relationship counselling? What is sex therapy?

- Sexual issues for youth/youth workers

- Who looks after the minister?

- Who looks after the minister's wife/husband?

- Disciplining after sexual sin
- Marriage preparation
- Designing a marriage prep course
- Sex & young people: The issues
- Emerging relationship help: 999
- Same sex attraction issues

Email: gary.g.mcfarlane@blueyonder.co.uk

www.garymcfarlane.com

Tel: (+44) 786 609 7247.